GEORGIA DISCOVERED

GEORGIA DISCOVERED

Exploring the Best of the Peach State

Written and Photographed by
CHRIS GREER

Globe Pequot

GUILFORD, CONNECTICUT

This book wouldn't have been possible without all of the love and support from my wife, Valerie. I traveled often and spent long days at the computer, and will be forever grateful for the time she spent taking care of our sons, Hayes and Brooks.

Globe
Pequot

An imprint of The Rowman & Littlefield Publishing Group, Inc.
4501 Forbes Blvd., Ste. 200
Lanham, MD 20706
www.rowman.com

Distributed by NATIONAL BOOK NETWORK

British Library Cataloguing in Publication Information available

Library of Congress Cataloging-in-Publication Data available

ISBN 978-1-4930-4537-2 (paper : alk. paper)
ISBN 978-1-4930-4538-9 (electronic)

♾™ The paper used in this publication meets the minimum requirements of American National Standard for Information Sciences—Permanence of Paper for Printed Library Materials, ANSI/NISO Z39.48-1992.

CONTENTS

DALTON

GAINESVILLE

ROSWELL

ATHENS

ATLANTA

AUGUSTA

GEORGIA

MACON

WARNER
ROBINS

COLUMBUS

SAVANNAH

ALBANY

WAYCROSS

VALDOSTA

WELCOME

Welcome to Georgia, a state rich with beauty, culture, and classic Southern charm. While there are other states that offer the unique combination of mountains and coast, the ease of travel and cost of living in Georgia provide a level of accessibility that visitors and residents truly appreciate. You can savor your morning coffee in the Blue Ridge Mountains and then enjoy fresh shrimp on Jekyll Island, all in the same day without battling mind-numbing traffic or paying an exorbitant amount of money.

Originally from Tennessee, I have lived in Georgia for the past fifteen years and truly do think of it as my home. I have been involved in several projects that have taken me all over the state, and in the process I have gained a genuine appreciation for all that is offered in the Peach State. It is diverse, both culturally and geographically, but a commonality throughout the far reaches of Georgia is the friendly and welcoming nature of its residents.

There are certainly other travel books available, ones that cover the cities and towns in greater detail. But this is different. Here I use my photographs to convey the rich beauty and wonder of the state to the reader. If a picture is worth a thousand words, then this book speaks volumes about the sublime beauty you will find throughout Georgia. These pages highlight the very best there is throughout the state, with a focus on all of the unique and alluring aspects of both the cities and the countryside. I have not only used my own extensive travels to curate the offerings in this book, I have also used the knowledge of Georgians from all over the state. Georgians who live, eat, work, and play in towns small and large, who know where the tourist traps are and also the hidden gems that can't be spotted from an interstate or four-lane highway. This is Georgia at its very best, and I hope you get a chance to enjoy these locations as I have.

—Chris Greer

Alluring pathways wind throughout the dense forest on Cumberland Island.

INTRODUCTION

Exploring the state of Georgia is a voyage of discovery. There is so much to see, do, and experience that even its residents can spend a lifetime trying to do it all. Some call it the "Peach State" while others refer to it as "Empire State of the South," but almost everyone agrees that Georgia has an enviable balance of culture and natural grandeur that is pervasive throughout its almost 60,000 square miles. Atlanta is the heart of the state, with almost six million people living within the sprawling metropolitan area. World-class dining, entertainment, art, and sports bring visitors from around the globe, and while you can spend weeks enjoying this thriving metropolis, you haven't really discovered Georgia until you have hit the road.

There are two main arteries in the state: Interstate 75 and Interstate 20. They provide rapid access to every border, but with them comes traffic and urban development. So when you can, take the backroads and appreciate the architecture and history in the town squares that can be strikingly similar yet beautifully unique. Almost every town has a similar layout—a stately courthouse surrounded by old buildings and locally-owned shops. There are so many towns in Georgia that it isn't possible to include all of them in this book, but even the tiniest bring a sense of wonder and simple splendor, with glimpses into once-thriving economies buoyed by cotton and tobacco. Many of these towns have grown quiet over the past half-century; interstates have absorbed the in-a-hurry tourists who used to flood the smaller state roads. The buildings remain, along with railroad tracks and old train depots that facilitated travel from these smaller settlements into the larger cities.

Agriculture has been a major contributor to Georgia's economic prosperity since the state was settled in the 1730s. While cotton remains, the once-thriving tobacco industry has given way to new heavy hitters, including peanuts, pecans, peaches, and blueberries. The prevalence of agriculture has led to a new cottage industry— agritourism. Every region of the state offers agritours that encompass everything from world-class wine to those oh-so-sweet Vidalia onions.

A different kind of prosperity has emerged over the past decade, one that has transformed the movie industry and the economy of the state. More major motion pictures now come out of Georgia than Los Angeles, with massive studios being constructed near Atlanta and a constant influx of actors and actresses stepping off airplanes to star in productions all over the state. The film industry invests billions of dollars every year in the state, and the result is tentpole productions such as *The Hunger Games*, *Stranger Things*, and *Avengers Infinity War*.

Freezing fog rises and falls over mountain peaks rich with fall colors.

Geographically, the topography in Georgia is never boring. Starting at the picturesque coastline, comprised of fourteen barrier islands and 368,000 acres of salt marsh, visitors can head north across a constantly changing landscape. The coastal plain provides massive views across fields that stretch as far as the eye can see. In prehistoric times, this was all covered by ocean, contributing to the flat terrain and sandy soil. Classic small towns emerge, some sleepy, some vibrant, but all historic. Moving north, hills begin to form as the soil transitions to predominantly red clay and then you arrive at the Piedmont. This transition zone is called the "Fall Line," which refers to the location where the ocean used to meet the land millions of years ago. Undulating countryside, large rock formations, and a mix of pine and hardwoods are all major features of the Piedmont region. Many of Georgia's largest cities are found here, including Atlanta, Augusta, Macon, Columbus, and Athens. Farther north, the hills get larger, the valleys deeper, and the Blue Ridge Mountains appear on the horizon. The northern part of Georgia consists of three distinct geographical regions: Blue Ridge, Ridge and Valley, and Plateau. One common feature runs through them all—mountains. While the northern neighbors of Tennessee and North Carolina are more often thought of when it comes to the Appalachians, Georgia does have its fair share. Stretching from the Alabama border all the way to South Carolina, the southern Appalachians bring a sense of calm along with their rich ecological diversity. With age comes wisdom, and at 480-million-years old these mountains are some of the wisest in the world. Their dense canopy shields the forest floor from the hot Georgia sun, protecting a sensitive and diverse ecosystem that is home to a multitude of flora and fauna.

Georgia is a state of contrasts, from mountains to the sea, from bustling shopping to the quiet solitude of the Appalachian Trail, from the bright city lights of downtown Atlanta to the dark-sky-certified shadows of the Okefenokee Swamp. It is a state full of adventure, peaceful tranquility, friendly Southern charm, and a melting pot of cultures from the far reaches of the globe. It is full of movie stars and directors filming blockbuster movies from the mountains to the coast, and hard-working people proud of their craft who will greet you with a warm handshake and a cold glass of sweet tea. This is Georgia, and it's time for you to discover it.

Libations

The popularity of craft beer and good wine is alive and well in the state of Georgia, perhaps in part due to the fact that both types of alcohol are fermented all over the state, and in large numbers.

As you might guess, there are simply too many breweries and wineries in the state to cover each with the needed depth to do them justice. Below you will find some notable vineyards and breweries found here in the Peach State. Additionally, each chapter of the book offers a list of breweries and wineries in the area. Hopefully this will provide you with a starting point to arrange a visit or two, no matter where your travels take you. Chances are you will be pleasantly surprised with the commitment to quality, and the resulting taste, that these establishments offer.

VINEYARDS

While craft beer can easily be brewed anywhere in the United States, the unique climate and topography of Georgia creates a niche for winemakers. From the mountains to the coast, you will find a variety of vineyards, helmed by experts who are constantly perfecting their craft.

Muscadine grapes are native to the United States and grow quite well in the hot and humid climates of the South. There are many people who appreciate not only the taste, but

Muscadine grapes can be found on vines almost anywhere in Georgia.

Rows of grapes await their harvest in late summer or early fall.

the historical importance of these grapes. They were used extensively by early settlers for winemaking, and some of the wine was sent back to Queen Elizabeth I for her own enjoyment.

While most visitors assume the wine in Georgia is primarily based on these muscadines, there are far more varieties of grapes and wines grown in the moderate climate of north Georgia.

DID YOU KNOW? Back in 1735, Georgia was the first colony to cultivate grapes.

Throughout south Georgia you will find vineyards making a variety of muscadine wines. As you make your way north, things begin to change. The Southern Piedmont and Appalachians usher in a new climate, new soil, and new varieties of wine. It is here that you will find a wide range of wineries growing European grapes, including Cabernet Sauvignon, Merlot, Chardonnay, and Pinot Gris. Many of these wineries look and feel like their counterparts in Europe, with rolling or mountainous terrain, large beautiful buildings, and tasting rooms that cater to even the most demanding wine enthusiast. In 2014 the state was given its first designated wine region, the Upper Hiwassee Highlands AVA, a 700-square-mile expanse that dwarfs Napa Valley. There are now more than forty wineries in the northern part of the state, and that number will continue to grow.

YONAH MOUNTAIN VINEYARDS, CLEVELAND

Sitting on 200 acres next to the rugged mountain for which it is named, this vineyard offers a tranquil setting with commanding views of the southern Appalachians. Inside the richly appointed tasting room is a large variety of wines waiting to be sampled.

The selection can be a bit overwhelming, but the highly knowledge-able staff will walk you through the tasting and educate you on the varieties. Make sure to sample the Meritage; it is a superbly blended wine made entirely from grapes grown on the property, and it will have you questioning all of your preconceptions about

You are in for a treat when you go for a tasting at Yonah.

wines in the Southeast. The winery is family-owned, offers live music on Saturdays, and is conveniently located between Cleveland and Helen. *yonahmountainvineyards.com, (706) 878-5522*

WOLF MOUNTAIN VINEYARDS, DAHLONEGA

Want to sample award-winning wines while enjoying a breathtaking view? You can't do much better than this winery, which sits at the top of Wolf Mountain and provides sweeping views of the Georgia mountains. This winery is large and ferments fantastic wines that have won numerous awards at prestigious wine competitions. If you try just one, make sure it is the Claret, a blend of Cabernet Sauvignon and Malbec that was aged for two years. After your tasting, grab a bite to eat at the café and sit outside to soak in the views and fresh mountain air. *wolfmountainvineyards.com, (706) 867-9862*

TIGER MOUNTAIN VINEYARDS, TIGER

Recognized regionally and nationally for its excellent wines, this vineyard offers a wide range of reds and whites, as well as some excellent food at the picturesque Red Barn Café. While the Malbec and Rosé are easy to drink and have widespread appeal, it is their Petit Manseng that brings home the awards almost every year. There are also monthly gourmet dinners with visiting chefs, so call ahead and arrange a visit for some excellent food paired with a few glasses of wine. *tigerwine.com, (706) 782-4777*

FROGTOWN CELLARS

Just before you enter the high elevation of north Georgia, you'll find the gorgeous, rolling hills of Frogtown Cellars vineyard. Founded in 1998, the winery offers a large selection of wines and has received more than 200 medals for its efforts. Visitors can sample a wide

Rolling hills lead to distant mountains at Frogtown Cellars.

range of varieties as well as satisfy their hunger at the Italian Bistro, where everything is made on site. The tasting room provides six different combinations of tastings, ensuring every visitor is satisfied no matter their preference. *frogtown.com, (706) 865-0687*

CRAFT BREWERIES

Over the past decade, there has been a seismic shift in the brewing and consumption of beer throughout the United States. Statistics show that younger beer drinkers are demanding more choice, and quality, from their brews, and craft breweries have stepped up to answer the call. The result is an explosion of breweries across the country, with more than 7,000 now operating, satisfying the demand from beer-loving consumers. Not to be left out, Georgia is seeing a rapid growth in new breweries, due in part to a recent change in the distribution laws, with over seventy breweries now calling the Peach State home.

While the definition of "craft beer" has been debated, typically it is beer brewed using innovative methods from small, independent breweries that produce less than six million barrels per year.

SWEETWATER BREWING COMPANY, ATLANTA

This might be the most recognizable name in Georgia, with a nation-wide distribution and multiple awards for its concoctions. While SweetWater 420 is the most popular offering, visitors who step through the doors are treated to a wide range of styles. Located just north of downtown Atlanta,

There is always something new on tap at Sweetwater Brewing.

SweetWater hosts numerous events throughout the year when it isn't busy winning awards at the Great American Beer Festival. *sweetwaterbrew.com, (404) 691-2537*

MONDAY NIGHT BREWING, ATLANTA

This brewery has garnered recognition around the state and across the country as a brewer of high-quality ales that pair well with almost any food or social setting. One of their best is the Han Brolo American Pale Ale, which recently won best pale ale from *Paste Magazine*. The Midtown tasting room has a laid-back vibe with plenty of picnic tables and cornhole games to enjoy while sampling a wide range of styles from the taps. *mondaynightbrewing.com, (404) 352-7703*

REFORMATION BREWERY, WOODSTOCK

Downtown Woodstock has a lot to offer, but for beer lovers the first stop should be this brewery, a favorite throughout the state. Like many craft breweries, Reformation got its start from two home brewers who couldn't drink all their fermented creations. Fast forward five years and the beer has developed a substantial following around the Southeast, contributing to the 2018 opening of their impressive new brewery in Woodstock. A large deck and outdoor beer garden ensure plenty of space for beer connoisseurs to congregate in nice weather, and two large beer bars provide a respite from the rain or cold. There are many varieties on tap; if you like Belgian ales, then Jude is a must-try. *reformationbrewery.com, (678) 341-0828*

CREATURE COMFORTS, ATHENS

There are few breweries in the state that have generated more attention over the past few years than Creature Comforts. The owners purchased this 13,000-square-foot building, which was used to sell Chevys in the 1940s and is conveniently located in downtown Athens, and converted it into a beautiful brewery and tasting room.

A fantastic renovation transformed this old car dealership into a beautiful brewery.

It wasn't long before the highly successful Tropicalia IPA started winning awards and garnering a cult-like following. *creaturecomforts beer.com, (706) 410-1043*

OCONEE BREWING COMPANY, GREENSBORO

Located in downtown Greensboro, a prototypical small southern town, this brewery offers plenty to taste and a beautiful spot in

This award-winning brewery brings a bit of nightlife to Greensboro.

which to do it. Step inside this wonderfully restored mill warehouse from the 1900s (the owners won an award from the Georgia Trust for Historic Preservation) and gaze upon the numerous taps as well as the sparkling stainless-steel fermenters situated just behind them. While most famous for their Hey Man Blonde Ale, they offer a range of styles that satisfy even the most demanding beer lover. *oconeebrewingco.com, (706) 920-1177*

OMAHA BREWING COMPANY, OMAHA

This up-and-coming brewery is proof you don't have to open up shop in the middle of a city to put yourself on the map. The country roads south of Columbus are mostly farmland and pine trees, and this brewery is definitely off the beaten path. Yes, the tiny town of Omaha doesn't look like much, but if you take the time to drive down the long gravel driveway leading to this brewery you are in for a treat. A building originally constructed as a school in the 1940s is the centerpiece of the brewery. Perhaps the underground spring on the property is the secret behind all their tasty brews, including the fantastic Generals Select Stout. If you are planning to visit the highly recommended Providence Canyon, then this brewery isn't too far up the road. *omahabrewingcompany.com, (229) 838-4779*

MOON RIVER BREWING, SAVANNAH

Beer taps aren't the only things that go bump in the night in this haunted brewery located in the enchanted historic district of Savannah. Considering the history of the building, it isn't that surprising. Built in 1821 and used as a hospital during some truly terrible yellow fever outbreaks, the building is now known for great beer and spooky stories. In fact, it is so haunted that it even serves as a stop on the local ghost tour. Make sure you sip the Wild Wacky Wit, a gold medal winner that is way too easy to drink. Just don't go down to the basement alone—you never know what supernatural spirit you might find. *moonriverbrewing.com, (912) 447-0943*

If you're afraid of ghosts, you might want to stick to the spacious patio at Moon River.

ABOUT THIS BOOK

This book is a culmination of decades of photography experience combined with a sense of wanderlust and adventure. It was crafted with love, through thousands of miles of travel, early alarms, late nights, tons of research, and the constant interaction with the warm and friendly residents who live throughout the state. It aims to be a different kind of travel book, one that captures the very best of Georgia, not only through words and descriptions, but through artistic imagery that elevates above snapshot photography and into the realm of fine art. The photographs in this book are the result of hundreds of hours of driving, location scouting, permission requests, and overcoming the various elements that Mother Nature threw my way. While admittedly not every one of the photos you find throughout these pages are worthy of being hung on a wall, my goal was to capture the beauty of Georgia in a way that does it justice, showcasing the natural splendor that stretches from the mountains to the coast and all points in between.

Georgia consists of distinct geological provinces, and some of those were used to provide context and organization to this rather large state. A few liberties were taken with the actual defining lines of each area, primarily to keep things easy to find as well as to facilitate day trips to different regions of the state. Each section

highlights a variety of towns, cultural destinations, recreational opportunities, as well as some unique points of interest that don't always fall neatly into a single category. The hundreds of locations outlined in this work are organized from north to south and east to west. This ensures that if you are driving and exploring, each entry will be in close geographical proximity to the ones around it.

The great outdoors are near and dear to me and that strong influence is reflected in this book. While a large majority of the locations have an outdoor component, some are heavily geared toward those who enjoy being outside. Many of the recommended destinations are a showcase of the numerous parks and other natural areas that provide recreational opportunities to visitors of all ages. Most are either free or have a very small entrance fee, ensuring access to everyone while still preserving the beauty and conservation that is so needed in these days of urban sprawl and scorched earth developments. In order to easily distinguish locations, a small 🦬 icon has been added for those that offer excellent outdoor recreation.

As with any creative project, some might insist that certain content should have been included or left out, depending on personal opinions and experiences. My main ambition was to travel the state and find the places that offer an engaging and memorable experience to the visitor, as well as unique and authentically Georgia. With only a few exceptions, this book does not include any mention of national chains or franchises in regard to any of the businesses highlighted. Because of numerous online resources for finding and booking accommodations, hotels are not mentioned or recommended unless they are exemplary and provide an experience that is exceptional and rare. Some restaurants are highlighted, primarily because they are locally-owned and wholeheartedly recommended by the residents who dine there often.

Before I started this project, I was fortunate enough to have a social media following that provided me with access to a multitude of insights and recommendations that aren't afforded to a typical travel writer. I live in Georgia, as do thousands of my followers, and their voices and recommendations helped me shape the book into a creation that reflected the local hot spots and hidden gems that don't always appear with a Google search. One of my favorite things in the world is photography, and when I began working on this book I committed to taking every photo that would be in it. I know many of you also enjoy taking photos, so I have highlighted the most photo-genic locations with a 📷 icon.

Best BBQ in Georgia

There are staples you find in the southeastern United States—SEC football, dirt roads, big pickup trucks, boiled peanuts, and plenty of BBQ. While some of these might not appeal to you, it seems that BBQ is enjoyed by almost everyone, and even vegetarians can find some sides to satisfy their hunger. So you're in luck when you are traveling around Georgia, because great BBQ can be had practically anywhere in the state. The following places have exceptionally good pork that has earned them a stellar reputation in the Peach State and beyond. They are listed in no particular order, because it is almost impossible to rank these establishments, which all exude excellence with their smoked meats.

Fresh Air BBQ, Jackson and Macon

While there is now a second location in Macon, the original Fresh Air BBQ restaurant is almost pilgrimage-worthy. Established in 1929, there are few other BBQ restaurants in the country that have been around for almost a century. The place is old, which adds to the charm and authenticity. If the walls of this wooden structure could talk, it would be with a raspy voice because they have housed a massive smoker for longer than most of us have been alive. Walk through the doors and you are greeted by classic photos on the wall and the smell of burning wood as it slowly and methodically cooks a variety of meats. A vinegar-based sauce is simple and perfect, even for those who normally prefer the tomato variety. *freshairbarbecue.com, (770) 775-3182*

Hours of smoking results in mouth-watering flavor for the customers.

Southern Soul Barbeque, Saint Simons Island

It's almost not fair that the residents and visitors on this idyllic island on Georgia's coast get to enjoy sea breezes, beautiful sunrises, and some of the best BBQ in the state. But hey, maybe it's all the more reason to go dip a toe in the ocean before you eat some mouth-watering pulled pork or brisket. Crowned the South's Best Smokehouse two years in a row by *Southern Living Magazine*, even BBQ competition judges find plenty to love in this converted old gas station. Wash your ribs down with a craft beer and call it a day . . . a very, very good day. *southernsoulbbq.com, (912) 638-7685*

Fox Bros. Bar-B-Q, Atlanta

Creative menu items and consistent quality have helped this restaurant set the standard for BBQ in the Atlanta metro area. Since their restaurant opened in 2007, Jonathan and Justin Fox have been smoking all kinds of meats to the delight of residents and visitors from near and far. Lots of outdoor patio space make this

The patio at Fox Bros. is a popular spot on a beautiful day.

a thriving destination on a pretty day, but no matter when you show up, there might be a bit of a wait. It's worth it though, because menu items like *The Terminator* (tater tots with Brunswick stew and cheddar cheese) have put this establishment on the map, with help along the way from features on TLC, HGTV, and the Food Network. *foxbrosbbq .com, (404) 577-4030*

B's Cracklin' Barbecue, Atlanta and Savannah
While Fox Bros. has long set the standard for excellent BBQ in Atlanta (and beyond), Bryan Furman has taken the scene by storm with his excellent pit-smoked BBQ. You'll find not only pork, but plenty of chicken and ribs on the menu at both locations, along with classic sides like collard greens and mac & cheese. Most restaurants could hardly survive one, let alone two, fires (one at the Savannah location and one in Atlanta) but the communities rallied around Furman to ensure his smoked meats are around for years to come. facebook.com/BsCracklinBBQATL/, *(678) 949-9912*

Jim's Smokin' Que, Blairsville
Check the parking lot Thursday through Saturday (the only days Jim's Smokin' Que is open) and you immediately know the food is good. License plates from all over Georgia and beyond are proof that this BBQ is worth the drive, and if that's not enough then look at the line out the door. When it opened in 2011 word quickly spread that this was no ordinary smokehouse. Whether it's the top-secret sauce or the cherry wood that's used for the smoke, you are guaranteed to have a flavorful experience here in the high elevations of Georgia. If you want to ensure the full menu is available, don't wait until late to show up because they do sell out. *jimssmokinque.com, (706) 835-7427*

A line out the door is a common sight when you pull up to Jim's.

Gary Lee's Market, Brunswick
There is nothing fancy about this BBQ joint, which is more of a butcher shop with counter service. But make no mistake, they take their BBQ seriously and this unassuming building houses some of the best BBQ on the coast. An easy stop off of Interstate 95, Gary Lee's Market offers excellent pulled pork and a brisket sandwich that is well worth your time. They serve wings and burgers as well, but it would be almost criminal if you didn't sample the BBQ and sauce. *(912) 265-1925*

Fall colors are everywhere in October and early November.

NORTH GEORGIA

If you start from the northwest corner of the state, you find yourself on the Appalachian Plateau, also known as the **Plateau region**. This portion of the Appalachian Mountains extends from north Alabama all the way to New York. Although this region is the smallest province in Georgia, it holds a great deal of beauty. Mountains rise into the air and coal can be found under the earth's surface, the only place in Georgia where it forms. A primary feature of the area is the pervasive sedimentary rock that was formed by the deposition and cementation of materials such as minerals, sand, and other rocks. This all comes together to create an interesting and dynamic landscape.

Like in many other sections in this book, the following locations are not all found perfectly within the official Plateau province; however, it is the dominating geological feature in this part of the state. Its close proximity to both Atlanta and Chattanooga make it a popular destination for residents of Georgia, Tennessee, and places far beyond.

Traveling east you eventually reach the **Blue Ridge**, which is located in the northeastern region of Georgia and features the highest mountains in the state. The Blue Ridge Mountains start in Georgia and stretch all the way to southern Pennsylvania. This region of Georgia consists of approximately 1,850 square miles and features striking scenery, cooler temperatures, and a more temperate climate. Some incredibly old rocks are found in this region, ranging from four hundred million to over one billion years old. The Blue Ridge Mountains are part of the Appalachian Mountain range, which forms the Eastern Continental Divide. The Divide separates watersheds draining into the Atlantic Ocean from those draining into the Gulf of Mexico, meaning a stream that runs down the eastern side of the Appalachian Mountains will eventually empty into the Atlantic Ocean, and a stream that runs down the western face of the Appalachians will empty into the Gulf of Mexico.

Due to the high elevation, the Blue Ridge Mountains cool the warm air currents brought in from the Gulf of Mexico. This results in abundant precipitation, which aids the river flow for the Chattahoochee and Savannah rivers. Summer thunderstorms are common among the high mountain peaks of this area, popping up and disappearing frequently while providing needed moisture to keep the landscape lush and green.

Perhaps rivaled only by the Georgia coast, the beauty of this region is hard to capture in photographs or words; it needs to be seen and experienced. Small winding roads carve their way through the mountains, usually alongside a stream that has slowly and methodically eroded the hard rock surface of the mountain and

Late day sun streaks across the mountain tops near Clayton.

produced a small valley that provides a habitat for many plant and animal species. Small towns dot the landscape, some without even a stoplight to slow the passing traffic. These towns might not be incorporated, but generations of families have lived there long enough that their last names have been used for the naming of the small roads and lanes in the area.

Grand vistas from mountain overlooks let visitors gaze to Alabama, Tennessee, North Carolina, and even South Carolina. These layers of peaks and valleys fill the sky and invoke a sense of calm, belonging, peace, and appreciation for just how small we are amongst the vast landscape. Storms pass in the distance, their rains partially obscuring some mountains while others remain clearly visible. It is a landscape of contrasts—temperature changes, shaded pathways, burbling streams, quiet roads, and sprawling farmland that eventually cedes to the harsh topography of these ancient mountains. The mountains are a jewel for the state of Georgia, and even with the seemingly unending population of nearby Atlanta, there is still plenty of peace and quiet to be had no matter the time of year.

Transitioning south from the highest elevations of Georgia brings you down to the **Piedmont,** which is vast, providing an expansive transition from the sandy soil of the coastal plain (pre-historic Georgia used to have a much larger coastline and far less inhabitable land) to the foothills of the Appalachians. The foothills have a beauty to them that is subtle, yet highly enjoyable. Rolling terrain stretches to the horizon while a rich mix of hardwood trees provide flowers in the spring, shade in the summer, and beautiful colors in the fall. A mix of medium and small cities are scattered throughout the area, with the vibrant city of Athens serving as the anchor from which a variety of day trips (or even overnights) can be had. So, while the foothills might not have the same cachet of the Appalachian Mountains, they are not to be overlooked. Listen to some music, eat some fantastic food, stroll through picturesque downtowns, and pick out an antique or two.

The sound of falling water brings visitors to the picturesque Helton Creek Falls.

Hemlock Falls is worth the hike at Moccasin Creek State Park.

A magical morning of fog.

Cows graze in a peaceful oasis of green, surrounded by the mountains.

Ice covered trees line a curvy road
in north Georgia.

📷 ROCK CITY, LOOKOUT MOUNTAIN

Even if you have never stepped foot in Georgia, you have probably heard of Rock City thanks to a tourism campaign that was a bit of marketing genius, long before the days of the Internet and viral videos. For those unaware, more than 900 barns were painted with the slogan "See Rock City" between 1935 and 1969, spanning states as far away as Michigan. Many of these barns have since become dilapidated piles of wood, but the tourist attraction lives on. While some might decry it as a "tourist trap" (it does get rather crowded, especially on weekends), others see it as a cultural icon, mixed with a bit of history and a lot of beauty. Lover's Leap waterfall is the main showpiece, cascading over a hundred feet down the sheer rock face of the mountain. For many, just being able to say they "Saw Rock City" is worth the price of admission. *seerockcity.com, (706) 820-2531*

There are still plenty of barns that advertise the iconic Rock City.

CHICKAMAUGA AND CHATTANOOGA NATIONAL MILITARY PARK, FORT OGLETHORPE

Civil War battles occurred throughout the eastern United States, but the state of Georgia had several that were very consequential. Perhaps the most critical conflict was located here, on the border of Georgia and Tennessee. The National Park Service preserves this pivotal battle site of the war between the North and the South. Nearby Chattanooga was known as the "Gateway to the South" and military control of the city was essential to the desired outcome of the war. Confederates were able to retain control of Chickamauga after a bloody two-day battle with Union soldiers, resulting in almost 35,000 casualties (second

Lingering fog shows how Cloudland Canyon got its name.

only to Gettysburg) between the two sides. Union troops retreated to the north, but their continued control of Chattanooga heavily influenced the remainder of the war. *nps.gov/chch, (423) 821-7786*

📷 🦬 CLOUDLAND CANYON STATE PARK, RISING FAWN

A geologist's paradise awaits at this state park, which sits close to the Alabama and Tennessee borders. Its location on the edge of Lookout Mountains affords visitors views of multiple ridges, steep rocky ledges, fog-filled valleys, and an up-close look at the variety of rock that makes up these mountains. The park is massive, and within its acres you'll find many waterfalls, miles of hiking trails, deep gorges, and a selection of cottages. If you have the legs for it, take the Waterfalls Trail down to the bottom of the canyon where you will find the picturesque Cherokee Falls and Hemlock Falls. There is never a bad time to be in this park, but it is incredibly peaceful at night. There are multiple park benches along the edge of the mountain, providing easy access for some star-gazing or astrophotography. *gastateparks.org/CloudlandCanyon, (706) 657-4050*

📷 HOWARD FINSTER'S PARADISE GARDEN, PENNVILLE

This small tract of land is dedicated to the quirky and acclaimed artwork of Howard Finster, a retired Baptist preacher–turned folk artist who created colorful sculptures, paintings, and other eclectic works of art. While many artists get started early in life, Finster didn't begin his career until the age of fifty-nine, after receiving a spiritual revelation while repairing a bicycle in his workshop. What ensued was an astonishing 46,991 numbered works of art before his death at eighty-one years of age. The gardens consist of multiple large buildings on four acres of land, each filled with art of all sizes and materials. Wander the grounds, admire the five-story "Folk Art Chapel," and perhaps you will have a vision of your own. *para disegardenfoundation.org, (706) 808-0800*

ROME

This town of 36,000 people provides a much-sought-after mix of culture, beauty, and warm southern charm. It's small enough to explore on foot, yet large enough to capture, and hold, your attention. It could be a perfect base from which to travel and explore the many enticing locations in northwest Georgia. Downtown Rome has

Eclectic architecture and colorful art are the reasons people flock to Paradise Garden.

Downtown Rome offers a nice blend of shopping, dining, and some nightlife.

a classic feel of the South, with the added beauty of two rivers and the nearby Appalachians rising from the horizon. The Etowah and Oostanaula Rivers flow out of nearby mountains and converge to form the Coosa River in the heart of Rome. While the downtown area spans several square miles, you will want to get started on Broad Street, which sits two blocks from the Oostanaula River. Visitors have plenty to choose from here, with a variety of shopping and dining options available for all tastes and budgets. The nearby Town Green is a small greenspace right on the banks of the river, perfect for a picnic on a sunny day.

If you want to truly appreciate the beauty of the area, head up to the terraced Myrtle Hill Cemetery, which affords a beautiful view of the nearby mountains. You can also stroll over to the historic city Clocktower, which sits high atop a hill overlooking downtown. This historic structure is part water tank, part clock, and served as a water supply for the city of Rome up until 1960. Now it provides views along with a small museum. Lunch or dinner at the **Harvest Moon Café** (myharvestmooncafe.com, 706-292-0099) certainly won't disappoint, as the menu offers a wide variety

The historic Clocktower offers sweeping views along with a small museum.

DID YOU KNOW? Georgia is the second-largest state east of the Mississippi River. Its 60,000 square miles place it just shy of Florida, which has 5,000 more. Population-wise, Georgia ranks eighth nationally with a population of 10.5 million people. The population is concentrated mostly in the northern half of the state, with the south featuring wide stretches of farmland and a larger number of small, historical towns.

The Old Mill is a photographer's delight, even in poor weather.

of American food. If locally brewed beer is your thing, then walk down to **Rome City Brewing Company** (rome citybrewing.com, 706-584-7436) and sample a craft beer (try the Clocktower Double IPA if you're feeling frisky). Perhaps most importantly, you would be remiss if you didn't carve out some time to explore the largest college campus in the world.

Berry College (berry.edu, 706-232-5374) clocks in at over 27,000 acres in size with much of it designated as a Wildlife Management Area. The college is private but open to visitors and offers a strikingly beautiful setting to explore. Astute observers might recognize many of the buildings from a slew of Hollywood movies and television shows. Numerous hiking and cycling trails wind through the fields and forests on campus, including one to the picturesque House o' Dreams on the top of Lavender Mountain. Speaking of pictures, the Old Mill is a must-visit for photographers,

as it has become an icon in this part of Georgia. While this campus is too large to fully explore in one day, it offers seemingly endless opportunities for visitors to enjoy the great outdoors. *romegeorgia.org, (800) 444-1834*

FORT MOUNTAIN STATE PARK, CHATSWORTH

North Georgia is home to many state parks, including this 3,700-acre paradise near Chatsworth. Originally occupied by Cherokee Indians in the 1700s, the park is steeped in history and beauty. Hikers can explore more than 25 miles of trails, or hop on a horse and take a guided tour of waterfalls, burbling streams, and mountain vistas. There is also a 14-mile mountain bike trail that attracts riders from all over the Southeast. The centerpiece (and namesake) of the park is an 885-foot rock wall that zigzags along the peak. Come for the history, stay for the beauty, and

Libations in North Georgia

Alro
Sweet Acre Farms Winery
sweetacrefarms.com

Athens
Akademia Brewing
akademiabc.com

Athentic Brewing Co.
athenticbrewing.com

Creature Comforts
creaturecomforts.com

Southern Brewing Co.
sobrewco.com

Terrapin Beer Co.
terrapinbeer.com

Blairsville
Odom Springs Vineyards
odomspringsvineyards.com

Paradise Hills Resort and Spa
paradisehillsresort.com

Blue Ridge
Bear Claw Vineyards
bearclawvineyards.com

Blue Ridge Brewery
blueridgebrewery.com

Fannin Brewing Company
fanninbrewingcompany.com

Grumpy Old Men Brewing
grumpyoldmenbrewing.com

Braselton
Braselton Brewing
braseltonbrewing.com

Canon
Southern Origin Meadery
bluehavenbee.com

Canton
Green Line Brewing Company
greenlinebrews.com

Cartersville
Drowned Valley Brewing Company
drownedvalleybrewing.beer

Cleveland
CeNita Vineyards and Winery
cenitawinery.com

The Cottage Vineyard & Winery
cottagevineyard.com

Serenity Cellars
serenitycellars.com

Tantrum Brewing Company
tantrumbeer.com

Yonah Mountain Vineyards
yonahmountainvineyards.com

Cornelia
Whistle Top Brew Company
whistletopbrew.com

Dahlonega
Cavender Creek Vineyards and Winery
cavendercreekvineyards.com

Frogtown Cellars
frogtown.us

Kaya Vineyard and Winery
kayavineyards.com

Montaluce Winery
montaluce.com

Three Sisters Vineyards and Winery
threesistersvineyards.com

Wolf Mountain Vineyards and Winery
wolfmountainvineyards.com

Dalton
Dalton Brewing Company
daltonbrewing.com

Danielsville
Boutier Winery
boutierwinery.com

Dawsonville
BeeCraft Mead Co.
beecraftmead.com

Castell Vineyards and Winery
castellwinery.com

Ellijay
Cartecay Vineyards
cartecayvineyards.com

Cartecay River Brewing Company
cartecayriverbrewing.com

Engelheim Vineyards
engelheim.com

Ott Farms and Vineyard
ottfarmsandvineyard.com

Gainesville
Left Nut Brewing Co.
leftnutbrewing.com

Greensboro
Oconee Brewing Co.
oconeebrewingco.com

Hartwell
Southern Hart Brewing
southernhartbrewing.com

Helen
Habersham Winery
habershamwinery.com

Hiawassee
Hiawassee Brew
(706) 896-2739

Hightower Creek Vineyards
hightowercreekvineyards.com

Jasper
Fainting Goat Vineyards and Winery
faintinggoatvineyards.com

Sharp Mountain Vineyards
sharpmountainvineyards.com

Madison
Amici Livery
amici-café.com

Monroe
Major Humphreys
majorhumphreys.com

Southern Brewing Company
sobrewco.com

Morganton
Serenberry Vineyards
serenberryvineyards.com

Rabun Gap
12 Spies Vineyards
12spiesvineyards.com

Ringgold
Georgia Winery
georgiawines.com

Rock Spring
Phantom Horse Brewing
phantomhorsebrewing.com

Rome
Rome City Brewing Company
romecitybrewing.com

Sautee
Sylvan Valley Lodge and Winery
sylvanvalleylodge.com

Talking Rock
Chateau Meichtry
chateaumeichtry.com

Tiger
Stonewall Creek Vineyard & Winery
stonewallcreek.com

Tiger Mountain Vineyards
tigerwine.com

Toccoa
Curahee Vineyards
curaheevineyards.com

Villa Rica
Hixtown Brewing Company
hixtownbrewing.com

Young Harris
Crane Creek Vineyards
cranecreekvineyards.com

Climb to the top of one of the mounds to soak in the view.

Visitors to the Booth Western Art Museum will be treated to a wide variety of art.

get a lot of fresh air in the process. *gastateparks.org/fortmountain, (706) 422-1932*

ETOWAH INDIAN MOUNDS, CARTERSVILLE

Native Americans once resided all over the region, and there are still many tell-tale signs of their civilizations. One of the most impressive is this state historic site outside Cartersville. Though only 54 acres in size, it includes six mounds, ditches, a plaza, and a range of artifacts in the museum. Visitors can climb to the top of the largest mound, which is 63 feet high and provides views of the distant mountains. Afterwards, stroll down to the scenic Etowah River, which runs through the back of the property and still contains the rocky fish traps used by Native Americans. *gastate parks.org/etowahindianmounds, (770) 387-3747*

BOOTH WESTERN ART MUSEUM, CARTERSVILLE

You might think that you need to trek out to Utah or Arizona to experience the art and stories of the Wild West, but you will be hard-pressed to find a better offering of Western art than at the Booth Western Art Museum. This award-winning museum wants visitors to come "See America's Story" and features more than 120,000 square feet of exhibit space. You can explore a wide variety of art and visual treasures, including a gallery of hand-signed letters from every US President; a gallery dedicated to the Civil War; and Sagebrush Ranch, an interactive exhibit for children ages 2 through 12. *boothmuseum.org, (770) 387-1300*

FUNK HERITAGE CENTER, WALESKA

Georgia was once home to a large population of Native Americans, and this museum is committed to preserving the culture and heritage of the Southeastern Indians. Located on the campus of Reinhardt University, the center features striking Native American architecture, a fascinating film about their civilization, and an extensive collection of artwork and artifacts. The National Park Service Trail of Tears has designated the site as a certified interpretive center, a testament to the comprehensive experience that is available to all visitors. *reinhardt.edu/funkheritage, (770) 720-5970*

GIBBS GARDENS, BALL GROUND

Botanists, gardeners, artists, and outdoor-lovers all agree—this is an absolute gem and well worth a visit. More than 200 acres of world-class gardens are open for the public to explore, with vivid flowers, rare trees, burbling brooks, and an intoxicating smell that only Mother Nature can provide. The gardens include 24 ponds, 32 bridges, and 19 waterfalls that provide a symphony of sound to accompany the visual feast throughout the sprawling grounds. *gibbsgardens.com, (770) 893-1881*

COHUTTA WILDERNESS, CISCO

If wild rivers, challenging trails, and solitude is what you seek, then the Cohutta is your answer. Over 37,000 acres of mountainous beauty await, along with 90 miles of trails, tons of creek crossings, and backcountry camping that attracts adventurers from all over the country. The Cohutta is rugged, beautiful, and can provide a soul-cleansing experience for avid outdoor lovers. Waterfall lovers will not leave disappointed, as

Thousands of daffodils bring spectacular color to the gardens every spring.

cascades can be found throughout the wilderness. If you have time for the hike, Jacks River Falls is particularly striking. Cell service is spotty and trails are remote, so make sure to tell someone where you are going and when you plan to be back.

BLUE RIDGE AND NEIGHBORING TOWNS

The bustling mountain town of Blue Ridge has something for everyone, including fine dining, excellent shopping, and a vintage train that makes daily trips to the mountains of Tennessee. Most of the highlights are found along East and West Main

Brilliant light sweeps over the colorful Cohuttas in the fall.

streets in the downtown area. The city hosts festivals throughout the year and can serve as a great home base from which to explore the surrounding elevations. If you want to experience the mountains using non-traditional transportation, take the **Blue Ridge Scenic Railway** (brscenic .com, 706-632-8724) up to nearby McCaysville for lunch. Once you arrive back in Blue Ridge, do some shopping, eat some ice cream at **MooBears** (moobearsicecream.com, 706-276-2611), sign up for fly-fishing lessons at **Fly Fish Blue Ridge** (flyfishblueridge .com, 706-455-5640), and enjoy some live music and a refreshing beer at **Blue Ridge Brewery** (blueridgebrew ery.com, 706-632-6611). It seems no matter what direction you drive in, you'll find plenty of beauty along the way. One particularly special drive is

the twisty Highway 60 that runs from nearby Morganton down to Suches, which sits at almost 3,000 feet in elevation and offers mild temperatures, even in the heart of summer.

The railroad is the epicenter of lively downtown Blue Ridge.

Len Foote Hike Inn

High in the mountains, miles from civilization, sits an oasis of fresh air, spectacular views, and unflinching sustainability. Named after the leading conservationist and biologist Lenoard E. Foote, the Len Foote Hike Inn opened its doors in 1998. It is not your typical mountain lodge, instead it caters to those who want to combine a beautiful hike with a few comfortable necessities and to unplug from society for a night or two. It turns out that there are plenty of people who seek this kind of experience. The inn serves more than 9,000 guests per year, meaning advance reservations are a necessity. Guests make the 5-mile trek up to the lodge, and once there they sit back and relax while appreciating the commitment to sustainability and conservation. Hot showers are available thanks to the solar panels on the roof. Leftover food is quickly disposed of into large containers containing numerous red wiggler worms, part of the vermiculture program that ensures nothing is wasted. Any rain that falls is preserved, filling barrels that can be used to water the gardens that surround the property. Perhaps one of the most visually striking parts of the

Get away from it all at the Len Foote Hike Inn.

lodge, other than the fascinating architecture, is the overlook and accompanying Star Base that provide excellent views to guests who relax in the Adirondack chairs. The Star Base was designed by Atlanta's Fernbank Science Center and aligns with the sun during the spring and fall equinoxes. While the accommodations would never be described as luxurious, guests are provided with meals and a comfortable bed, along with warm water and electricity. You aren't there for luxuries after all; you are there for the natural surroundings, the fellowship of other outdoors lovers, and the crisp, cool air that the 3,100-foot elevation provides. *hike-inn.com, (800) 581-8032*

Several rushing creeks as well as the massive Coopers Creek WMA are nearby, providing tons of fishing and hiking opportunities. A little closer to Blue Ridge is the town of Aska, which sits near the banks of the scenic Toccoa River. Hiking trails, waterfalls, and the rushing river all provide excellent outdoor opportunities no matter the time of the year. If you want to see a beautiful working farm that offers a wide variety of apples and other fruit, **Mercier Orchards** (mercier-orchards .com, 800-361-7730) is a fun destination for the entire family. Try the apple cider donuts; they are sinfully delicious. *blueridgemountains.com, (800) 899-6867*

📷 🏞 AMICALOLA FALLS STATE PARK, DAWSONVILLE

There is a lot to love about this state park located just north of Dawsonville. A massive, 729-foot waterfall is the centerpiece, with water rolling and tumbling over massive rocks and multiple ledges during its journey to the lower elevations. Of course, there are multiple hikes, all quite beautiful and varying in length. Perhaps more interesting though is the variety of lodging available in the park. A beautiful lodge, full of amenities and all of the creature comforts one needs, sits high on a hill near the falls (amicalola fallslodge.com, 706-344-1500, see sidebar). But the more adventurous might elect to stay at the LEED-certified Len Foote Hike Inn, which is only accessible by foot and provides a level of peace and tranquility that is rare in this day and age. A five-mile hike brings guests to the structure, which contains twenty rooms for guests and provides hot showers, fresh cooked meals, and a complete immersion into nature.

DAHLONEGA

If you aren't from Georgia, you might not associate the words gold rush with this region of the country. That term might conjure up thoughts of the Wild West, California, or even the state of Alaska, but Georgia has its own gold buried deep in the Appalachian Mountains. The second gold rush of the United States occurred here, near the town of Dahlonega. Prospectors from around the world descended on the area with dreams of striking it rich, much to the dismay of the Cherokee Indians who

The Gold Museum sits in the middle of downtown Dahlonega.

Paddlers float down the peaceful Chestatee River near Dahlonega.

inhabited the region. While there is still gold in those hills, the region is no longer a hotbed of mining activity. However, there is plenty of history and old mines to explore. If you want to learn about how it all started, visit the **Consolidated Gold Mine** (consolidatedgoldmine.com, 706-864-8473), which takes visitors 200 feet underground into a gold mine, giving you a chance to pan for your own gold. If you want to learn even more, head over to the **Gold Museum Historic Site** (gastateparks.org/Dahlonega GoldMuseum, 706-864-2257), smack in the middle of the beautiful downtown. Hungry? When you're done at the museum walk across the street to the charming **Picnic Café** (thepicnic cafe.wixsite.com/picniccafe, 706-864-1095) and grab a pimento cheese sandwich, considered a delicacy throughout the South. Downtown Dahlonega has plenty to keep you occupied, with great shops, ice cream, and a variety of dining options. The close proximity of North Georgia College & State University infuses culture and a youthful vibe into the town, and the nearby mountains keep the

air cool and conjure up thoughts of adventure. Speaking of which, **Chestatee River Adventures** (chestatee riveradventures.com, 770-540-9950) offers several options for floating down the scenic Chestatee, which lies just to the south of Dahlonega. If you'd rather stay dry, take Highway 19 north out of town, then bear left on Highway 60. You will enter a mountain paradise with epic views, peaceful trails, and the blissful Dockery Lake, which provides visitors plenty of

DID YOU KNOW? There have been many gold rushes throughout the history of the United States, but while many people associate California and Alaska with the shiny yellow metal, Georgia was the site of one of the earliest significant gold rushes in the nation's history. In the early 1800s, gold was found in multiple locations just east of Dahlonega, sparking an onslaught of prospectors who descended upon the area and drove off the Cherokee, eventually leading to the Trail of Tears.

solitude. At the end of the day, enjoy a bit of al fresco dining at the **Bourbon Street Grill** (thebourbonstreet grille.com, 706-864-0086). As the name implies, this restaurant specializes in food with a Cajun theme, and the beautiful setting might be as memorable as the food. If you want a bit of nightlife, stroll down to the **Crimson Moon** (thecrimson moon.com, 706-864-3982), a café that offers Southern food as well as live music several nights per week. *dahlonega.org, (706) 864-3711*

📷 BELL'S MOUNTAIN, HIAWASSEE

For those who don't like to hike but do like beautiful views, Bell Mountain is your place. It provides easy access to a 360-degree panoramic of the Appalachians and Lake Chatuge, one of the most beautiful lakes in north Georgia, and you don't have to hike to see it. A steep road leads to a parking lot just below the mountain summit.

From there you can access an observation platform that affords views in literally every direction. Contrasting with the rich beauty of the mountain, many of the rocks and boulders are covered with graffiti. This tradition started many years ago and continues to this day, even though many attempts have been made to thwart it. Some might like the bright vivid colors of the painted rocks, others might feel it is disrespectful and an eyesore. But all agree that the views from the top of Bell are some of the best in the state.

📷 🖼 BRASSTOWN BALD VISITOR'S CENTER, HIAWASSEE

It's pretty easy to identify the highest mountain in Georgia, because there is a large tower sticking up from its peak. The Brasstown Bald Visitor's Center provides visitors with the chance to experience a 360-degree panorama of mountains, providing

Panoramic views await visitors who tackle the steep road to the top of Bell's Mountain.

Valleys of fog stretch to the horizon under the watchful eye of Brasstown Bald.

long-range views of Tennessee, North Carolina, and South Carolina. From the parking lot, you can either take a shuttle or get your heart racing and tackle the steep half-mile trail to the summit. After you soak in the views and fresh air, head inside the museum to learn about the flora, fauna, and early settlers of the Southern Appalachian Mountains. A movie is shown every half-hour that showcases the seasonal beauty of the area, and there are plenty of other exhibits for visitors to enjoy. For avid hikers, there are several trails that run from the summit, including the serene Wagon Train Trail which winds down to nearby Young Harris. This trail passes through a vibrant and ecologically significant "cloud forest" on the northern slope of Brasstown Bald.

The regular fog and wet conditions in this area provide optimal growing conditions for lichen, ferns, and yellow birch trees. *(706) 896-2556*

SUNRISE GROCERY, BLAIRSVILLE

Nestled in a valley surrounded by some of the highest mountains in the state, this historical building first opened as a grocery in the early 1920s (it's the oldest remaining business in Blairsville). Named one of the "most charming general stores in the South" by *Southern Living* magazine, the store provides a little bit of everything to the thousands of visitors who walk through its wooden doors every year. Lots of local goods adorn the shelves, including dressings, jams, and a variety of arts and crafts. True to its name, there are even

The Appalachians

While they aren't the tallest mountains in the United States, the Appalachians are some of the oldest on Earth. Like a wise old man who comforts and teaches, so do these mountains that rise and fall from northern Alabama all the way to Maine. Many don't associate Georgia with mountains, but with peaks that near 5,000 feet above sea level, the state certainly has its fair share.

It is hard to wrap your brain around just how incredibly old these mountains are. While there is no perfect consensus on their age, many scientists estimate they were formed upward of 400 million years ago after an uplifting of sedimentary rock. Their height once approached that of the Rocky Mountains and perhaps even the Himalayas, dwarfing their modern-day elevation. Erosion for hundreds of millions of years can really do a number on those tall peaks, and the power of water has slowly and methodically worn the steep, rugged mountains down to their very cores.

The result is a mountain chain that is heavily forested and provides a habitat for an abundance of plant and animal species, some of which don't exist anywhere else on the planet. Interestingly, during prehistoric times, massive sheets of ice slowly descended southward from the northern Appalachians, scattering large boulders in their wake and driving plant and animal life into the southern part of the mountain chain. This accounts for the rich and unique biodiversity found throughout the mountains of Georgia, Tennessee, and North Carolina. Some of the largest broad-leaf deciduous forests can be found throughout these mountains, providing shade and shelter from the bottom of the

Blue Hole Falls lives up to its name, and is a favorite swimming hole for the locals.

Colorful mountains are shrouded by fog after heavy rains have finished.

Cows graze after a winter snow in north Georgia.

The morning sun casts shades of pink over fog-filled valleys.

A magical fall morning near Blairsville.

mountains all the way to their peaks. Scientists estimate that almost 200 species of Appalachian flora grow only within the southern Appalachians, punctuating the significance of the area and the unique biodiversity that is present.

The plants are just part of the diversity, because a wide range of animals also call these mountains home. Black bears roam the region, with the majority of their state-wide population (estimated at 5,100) being found in the mountains and foothills. In addition to these large animals, you might spot bobcats, coyotes, and red foxes during your travels. Let's not forget about the smaller animals either, because cute little critters like salamanders thrive in the temperate forests of the region. In fact, the Appalachian Mountains have a larger diversity of salamanders than any other location in the world. Some species are so rare that they can only be found in very small, distinct geographical areas, for example, the Pigeon Mountain Salamander exists only along the rock outcroppings and caves of Pigeon Mountain in northwest Georgia.

Today, visitors love to escape to these higher elevations of the Peach State in search of adventure, recreation, and perhaps some solitude. Outdoors lovers have a special affinity for and deference to these old mountains. Tall enough to provide snowfall in the winter and lush enough to provide plenty of shade in the summer, these mountains are never out of season. While the glorious colors of fall are certainly a highlight for the tourism industry in the patchwork of small towns that dot the landscape, many visitors prefer the other seasons that generally usher in smaller crowds and facilitate peaceful enjoyment of some of Mother Nature's greatest offerings.

Peaceful pathways wind throughout the Appalachians.

Kayakers explore the lake in Vogel State Park.

some groceries available, particularly popular with the throngs of campers coming from nearby Vogel State Park. If nothing else, stop and grab a bag of boiled peanuts—they sell five tons a year. *sunrisegrocery.com, (706) 745-5877*

VOGEL STATE PARK, BLAIRSVILLE

There are a lot of state parks in Georgia, and Vogel is one of the prettiest. The natural beauty and surrounding mountains make it very popular for campers as well as day-trippers. The 233-acre park is situated at the base of the mountains on Lake Trahlyta, and there is plenty for the entire family to see and do. Multiple trails satisfy the hikers, but if you want to relax and enjoy the sounds of a

burbling stream as it empties into the lake, grab a picnic table and gaze out over the water, which is likely peppered with kayakers or families in paddleboats. Along with the fishing and swimming, there's miniature golf, a few playgrounds, and lakeside cabins for rent. *gastateparks.org/vogel, (706) 745-2628*

RICHARD RUSSELL SCENIC HIGHWAY, HELEN

If you are in the area, this is a must-drive. This road undulates through steep mountains, over creeks, and past a variety of hiking trails. The drive is about 14 miles and takes you up and over Hogpen Gap, which also serves as a trailhead for the 2,190-mile Appalachian Trail. Pull off and soak in the views of the southern

Richard Russell Scenic Highway snakes through the colorful mountains of fall.

covered bridge spans the crystal clear Duke's eek in Smithgall Woods.

Appalachians that stretch to the horizon. During the winter months, a cliff of sheer ice forms, the result of spring water meeting the freezing cold air of the high elevations. If you are lucky you might spot a black bear; they roam the mountains of north Georgia and grow to 600 pounds or more.

SMITHGALL WOODS, HELEN

If you are looking for the anti-state park, then this is your destination. There is no lodge, no campground, no throngs of people splashing about on a manmade beach. There are a few quaint cottages and thousands of acres of natural splendor. This is carefully preserved nature, with some history sprinkled in. The fishing is world-class (catch and release only,

A yearly hot air balloon festival brings plenty of color to the lively city of Helen.

call ahead for reservations), with a trophy trout stream flowing right through the middle of the park. Even if you don't fish, the river is a jewel and the sound is simply intoxicating. Sit on the bank, eat a picnic lunch, then head off on one of the trails to get some fresh air or catch a glimpse at the honeybee hives on the property. You are almost guaranteed to feel relaxed and rejuvenated at the end of the day. *gastateparks.org/ smithgallwoods, (706) 878-3087*

HELEN

Helen is one of those towns that everyone should visit, even if it's not for everyone. Originally home to Cherokee Indians, then miners during the gold rush, the town truly transformed in 1969. It was then that three local businessmen decided that something should be done to capture the attention of tourists who were passing through the area into the more mountainous regions of north Georgia. The result? Helen was reinvented as a German village, with new facades installed all over the town. Fast-forward 60 years and Helen has

become a tourist mecca for those who want to escape the southern heat. The town offers all the requisite activities, including mini-golf, a waterpark, lots of shopping, and even more dining. If you find yourself in the area during September or October, you can't miss the crowds at Helen's Festhalle. It is the heart of the city-wide Oktoberfest celebrations, which (unlike in Germany) last for almost two months. Not a beer fan? By now you are probably well-aware of the award-winning wineries in this region of Georgia. If you feel like having a few glasses, then leave the driving to **VIP Southern Tours** (vipsoutherntours

DID YOU KNOW? If natural beauty is more your thing, take a short drive up the road to Anna Ruby Falls, a strikingly gorgeous confluence of two creeks that result in multiple waterfalls that can be observed from two viewing decks. These are some of the most popular waterfalls in the state, so avoid a weekend visit if possible.

Hundreds of tubes float down the Chattahoochee River every summer day in Helen.

.com, 706-348-8747). They have several offerings from downtown Helen, all visiting multiple wineries.

Far and away the most popular summertime attraction in Helen is floating down the Chattahoochee River in an oversized inner tube, also known as "shootin" the Hooch. There are three main companies that offer this service, which essentially involves transporting hundreds of visitors and colorful tubes upstream to facilitate an easy float down the river, which runs right through the middle of town (and under the watchful eye of patrons at the local watering holes). Depending on rainfall and the level of the river, you might find yourself dragging your tube over some of the rocks, but you are guaranteed to stay cool in the chilly water, even in the hottest summer months. *helenga.org, (706) 878-2181*

📷 ☁️ YONAH MOUNTAIN, CLEVELAND

Rising steeply from the hilly terrain outside of Cleveland, this mountain is a steep hike with a memorable payoff at the top. *Yonah* is the Cherokee word for "bear" and although there is always a chance you will happen across one of the thousands of black bears that reside in Georgia, it is a rare occurrence. After arriving at the parking lot, you begin the steep and rocky 2.3-mile trail to the top. This trail isn't for those who are out of shape, but if you complete the hike you are treated with a stunning view of the surrounding landscape. While there is a chance you will have it all to yourself, this mountain is popular with hikers, rock climbers, and even Army Rangers who do some training exercises nearby.

THE DILLARD HOUSE, DILLARD

In the very northern reaches of Georgia sits a swath of land with beautiful views and rich history. The Dillard family first settled the area in the late 1700s, eventually leading to the construction of the Dillard House in 1917. It has been renovated and added to over the years, with an inn, cottages, and the restaurant that brings

Rising high out of the surrounding landscape, Yonah offers views and a challenging hike.

Colorful leaves serve as a backdrop for the raging Chattooga River.

patrons from miles around. While the restaurant serves up breakfast, lunch, and dinner every day, it is that first meal of the day that might be the most famous. Meals at The Dillard House are something of an experience, as there is no menu from which you choose. The server brings out everything—literally everything—they are cooking for that meal and arranges it on the massive table in front of you, creating a veritable feast before your eyes. During breakfast that means meats, eggs, fruit, pastries, and even casseroles magically appear on the table, and you help yourself to anything you want. If you are still hungry, they just bring you more. The menu changes daily, so check their website before you head over, and bring a hearty appetite. *dillardhouse.com, (706) 746-5348*

📷 BULL SLUICE, CLAYTON

The Wild and Scenic Chattooga River is harsh, treacherous, and refuses to be tamed. Its rapids are the stuff of legend, with Class IV+ challenging even the most accomplished kayakers. If you love the feel of adrenaline pumping through your veins, take a guided trip down the river with the **Nantahala Outdoor Center** (noc.com, 828-785-4977). If you would prefer to watch others take the plunge (literally), you can park at Bull Sluice and walk down the path to the rocky overlook and watch kayakers and rafters attempt to navigate the heart-pounding rapids and remain in their craft. While the classic film *Deliverance* might have put this river on the map, its scenic beauty, mixed with the rugged terrain, is what brings visitors from all over the country, and the world.

CLAYTON

A true mountain town, Clayton is surrounded by the beautiful mountains of northeast Georgia and is a short drive from both North Carolina and South Carolina. If you want some food, like to shop, and enjoy being

The most famous and storied trail in the world begins its northward path in the Georgia mountains. The Appalachian Trail, commonly referred to as the "AT," twists and turns its way from Springer Mountain all the way to Mount Katahdin in the high elevations of Maine, covering 2,180 miles in all. Every spring a contingent of hikers from around the planet converge on Springer, all with one destination in mind. These thru-hikers aim to go for a walk in the woods and don't plan on stopping until they reach Katahdin, which can take upward of six months to accomplish. If they leave from Springer they are northbounders. The southbounders head toward Georgia from Maine, although they typically get a later start due to the unpredictably brutal weather on Katahdin. Those who don't have the vacation time, or willpower, to hike the whole thing at once, can still get credit for completing the AT by hiking it one section at a time.

There are multiple sections in Georgia, so maybe it's time for you to get started on your AT journey. No need for high-end gear. There are plenty of day hikes available for those who are in decent shape. All you

Black bears are found throughout the Appalachians, but are typically not aggressive.

need are comfortable shoes, a good supply of water, and maybe a granola bar. Below you will find a few of the popular (and scenic) AT trailheads in Georgia, with total mileage for the hike listed. Almost all of them have steep sections, but such is life in the Georgia mountains. In fact, many thru-hikers think of Georgia as one of the hardest parts of the trail due to near constant peaks and valleys. For more information about the many hiking trails of Georgia, take a look at the impressively comprehensive Atlanta Trails website (atlantatrails.com).

Blood Mountain (4.3 miles)

This is the highest peak on the AT in Georgia, and the payoff is a panoramic view of distant mountains and cities (you can even see the Atlanta skyline on a clear day). Popular on the weekends, the trail is pretty steep and not the best choice if you are out of shape or have any kind of mobility issues. Park just down the road at the Byron Reece trailhead, then take the spur trail from the parking lot up to the connection with the AT. At the summit you will find a stone structure built by the Civilian Conservation Corps (CCC) in the 1930s. It is popular with weekend hikers as well as thru-hikers who want a bit of shelter without erecting a tent. Soak in the views, then head back down the mountain and stop in at the Walasi-Yi Interpretive Center, the only spot where the AT passes through a man-made building. This building has served several functions in

The Blue Ridge Mountains often live up to their name.

The top of Blood Mountain provides sweeping views and an idyllic setting for hikers.

Part outfitter and part historical structure, Walasi-Yi sits high on a mountain.

Tread lightly and leave no trace when you are on the trail, as there is plenty of beauty underfoot.

Roots and fog make for a beautiful, and slippery, walk in the woods.

The endless mountains meet the setting sun.

its fascinating history, and today houses **Mountain Crossings** (mountaincrossings .com, 706-745-6095), an outfitter that caters to the constant influx of hikers who are just passin' through.

Tray Mountain (5 miles)

There are some steep sections on this hike, but your reward is a fantastic view of the northeast Georgia mountains. You will do about five miles in all if you leave from the parking area at Indian Grave Gap. The journey to the parking lot might be the hardest part for some, as the roads are gravel with plenty of ruts—low clearance vehicles might struggle. From your car, begin the journey up the mountain, passing through tunnels of rhododendron with fleeting glimpses of the surrounding mountains. There are occasional areas

that flatten out and let you catch your breath before the climb begins again. Reaching the ridgeline, continue to climb to the summit and enjoy the crisp air and cool breezes. You'll know you've arrived at the top when it opens up and the views are simply stunning.

Unicoi Gap (1.1 to the top, longer hike available)

Are you the type who likes a challenge? Then this is your trail. It is a steep and arduous climb from the parking area to Rocky Mountain, but the reward is well worth it, with the trail opening up to massive views of the mountains and distant Georgia piedmont. Though the trail is one of the most difficult, accessing it is incredibly easy. Highway 75 twists and turns on its journey from Helen to

Hundreds, if not thousands, of delicate streams await hikers on the AT.

Hiawassee, and you can't miss the parking area. From there you feel your heart pounding almost immediately as you ascend from the road up toward the summit. Small streams and backcountry campsites accompany you on the way to the top, where long-distance views of the tree-covered Appalachians await.

Preacher's Rock (2 miles)
Short and sweet, this might be the best AT hike for beginners in the entire state. Leaving from Woody Gap near Dahlonega, you are only on the trail for about a mile before you arrive at the large rock outcrop with beautiful long-range views. Perhaps one of the best things about this hike is that there are multiple views and overlooks that give you time to relax, sip some water, and soak in the layers of Appalachian Mountains that even the most hardened soul would find breathtaking.

Hogpen Gap (3 miles)
This small parking area can get a bit crowded on the weekends, though not quite as crowded as Blood Mountain. From here you can hike either direction, but if you want to do a shorter section with incredible views, hike south. From the parking area head across the road following the trail southwest toward Blood Mountain. The trail takes you up a small mountain and makes a sharp right, where you stay along a ridgeline for a bit of distance. You drop back down into a small valley and then head back up before reaching Cowrock Mountain, which has a very open panoramic view to the south.

Dicks Creek Gap (5.2 miles)
This moderate to difficult climb is the final easily accessible trailhead before the AT passes into North Carolina. The trail crosses Highway 76, which connects Hiawassee and Clayton, making it an easy drive from either town with parking right off the road. From your car, head south where the trail immediately starts to climb a slope rich with hardwood trees. After a half mile you get a brief respite before the final climb up to the top of Powell Mountain, where you are treated to sweeping views of the rolling mountains.

outside, this city ticks all those boxes and then some. Before you hit the area trails, make sure to wander in to **Wander North Georgia** (wandernorthgeorgia.com) to stock up on all of your outdoor needs, or just hang out and play a little cornhole in the back of the store (yes, it's inside, and yes, it's awesome). They can also point you in the direction of some fantastic hikes and scenery. Afterward, you might want to grab a bite to eat at **Universal Joint** (ujclayton.com, 706-782-7116), where you will find a nice range of food and a beautiful outdoor patio (they are very dog-friendly as well).

Heading out of downtown, just point your car and drive because no matter where you go, you'll be greeted by brilliant scenery and lots of wilderness. If you want to get some fresh air and exercise, the nearby Warwoman Dell Recreation Area as well as Chattahoochee National Forest will serve you well. After stretching your legs for a bit, head back to Clayton and decide if you feel like bourbon or wine. For the former, head to **Moonrise Distillery** (moonrisedistillery.com, 844-994-4759), where they produce bourbon, rye, and corn whiskey on site. Take a tour and sample their wares; you'll be impressed. Wine lovers should stroll in to **Noble Wine Cellar** (noblewinegeorgia.com, 706-212-0407) for a tasting in an

A peaceful mountain town, Clayton is a perfect spot to anchor your day trips.

Head down Warwoman Road to explore the rich forest.

Tallulah Gorge has some challenging hikes, but the views are worth it.

intimate and inviting space. If your appetite is ramping up, you can't go wrong with **Fortify Kitchen and Bar** (fortifyclayton.com, 706-782-0050). This award-winning farm-to-table restaurant offers culinary delights for even the pickiest eaters, providing a bit of Southern flavor in a slightly upscale setting. Reservations are likely needed for dinner, so plan accordingly. *explorerabun.com, (706) 212-0241*

📷 🌳 TALLULAH GORGE STATE PARK, TALLULAH FALLS

Who knew that one of the most visually impressive canyons in the eastern United States would be found in Georgia? One thousand feet deep and two miles long, the gorge is steep, rocky, and magical. The roaring Tallulah River tumbles and crashes its way through the gorge, and a series of waterfalls provides ample opportunities for photography and adventure. Adrenaline junkies from around the world descend upon the river twice a year for controlled releases of water from the nearby Tallulah Falls Dam, enjoying Class IV and V rapids that challenge even the most seasoned kayaker. For the rest of us, a hike to the canyon floor is plenty to get the heart pounding. Make sure you stop by the visitor center for your permit, as they only allow 100 per day. If hundreds of stairs sound a little too daunting, there are several overlooks at the top of the gorge that provide great views of the gorge and river below. *gastateparks.org/tallulahgorge, (706) 754-7981*

📷 📷 PANTHER CREEK FALLS, TURNERVILLE

If taking a solid hike and visiting a beautiful waterfall are your ideas of a great day, this should be on your itinerary. Located on the southern edge of the Georgia Appalachians, the waterfall is at the end of a moderately difficult 3.5-mile trail. Most

of the trail is up and down, with a few slippery areas that should not be attempted by those with mobility problems. The trail parallels a beautiful mountain stream for most of the way, providing a plethora of spots to catch your breath and cool off in the crystal-clear mountain water. The trail ends at a waterfall that is massive, thunderous, and very picturesque. This is a popular hike, but there is a fair amount of room at the bottom of the falls. You can easily spend hours wading in the water, exploring the sandy beach, or throwing up a hammock between a few of the numerous trees that border the water.

📷 TOCCOA FALLS, TOCCOA

One of the tallest free-falling waterfalls east of the Mississippi River is tucked away in this small town, and

Panther Creek Falls is a moderate hike, but the payoff is especially beautiful.

Uniquely tall with exceptionally easy access, it's easy to see why Toccoa Falls is so popular.

it is worth the drive. If you want to enjoy a majestic waterfall without a strenuous hike, then this should be on your short list. Located on the campus of Toccoa Falls College, the falls are easily accessible for anyone, including those in wheelchairs. There is a small fee to see the waterfall, payable at the nearby gift shop. If you are in the area, don't pass up the opportunity; this 186-foot high waterfall is impressive to see and to hear.

SHIELDS-ETHRIDGE HERITAGE FARM, JEFFERSON

Experience what it was like to live and work on a farm in the early 1800s at this wonderfully preserved showcase of historical agricultural buildings. The layout includes 18 buildings, ranging from a teacher's house to a gristmill.

Walk the grounds, explore the buildings, and let your mind wander back to a simpler time when everything was made by hand and transportation involved horses and carriages. After exploring this Southern farm, follow up with Southern comfort food at the **Carriage House** (carriagehousejeffer son.com, 706-367-1385), just a short drive up the road. *shieldsethridge farminc.com, (706) 367-2949*

HURRICANE SHOALS COUNTY PARK, MAYSVILLE

Nestled in the hills of Georgia's Piedmont, this county park is an undiscovered gem for many travelers. A short drive from Commerce brings you to the unassuming front entrance to the park, but within lies a beautiful cascading river and lots to explore.

Sit by the North Oconee and listen to the intoxicating sound as it crashes and tumbles over rocks and boulders, or take a hike on the nature trail to enjoy a bit of privacy. There is plenty to keep the kids occupied as well, from disc golf to mini golf, as well as a playground. For historical buffs, there is Heritage Village, which includes cabins, barns, and various other structures that have been preserved

exceedingly well. On a hot summer day, bring a swimsuit and inner tube. *hurricaneshoalspark.org, (706) 367-6350*

ATHENS

The Classic City is the cultural epicenter of the foothills region, an effusive heartbeat that pumps out music, art, food, and sports for the

A hidden gem in the northern Piedmont, Hurricane Falls has plenty of outdoor opportunities.

enjoyment of its residents as well as the hundreds of thousands who visit every year. The vibrant downtown is perched on a hill, overlooking the rolling landscape that leads to the southern Appalachians just 40 miles to the north. There are far more bars and restaurants than you can sample during your stay, but rest assured there is something for everyone. Iconic bands such as R.E.M, the B-52s, and Widespread Panic might have put Athens on the international map, but there is much more to this city than a thriving music scene. Take in an independent film at Cine, stroll through the immaculate State Botanical

Vibrant sunlight washes over downtown Athens.

Cars stream past on Broad Street between campus and downtown.

The setting sun casts a warm glow over the Botanical Gardens.

Gardens, sip a drink on the roof of the world-famous Georgia Theatre, and have a memorable dining experience at the award-winning 5&10 restaurant. Athens has a special quality that cannot be reproduced or contrived; it is simply a reflection of the thousands of happy and creative people who call it home. *visitathensga.com, (706) 357-4430*

📷 STATE BOTANICAL GARDENS, ATHENS

The official botanical gardens for the state of Georgia can be found a short drive from the bustling downtown. Nestled along the banks of the Middle Oconee River, the State Botanical Gardens showcase a mix of inspiring architecture and natural beauty. A beautiful indoor garden (complete with burbling stream) is a perfect appetizer for the main course outside: acres of manicured gardens, streams, hiking trails, and the Alice H. Richards Children's Garden. If you work up an appetite, there is also a café on site. Getting lost for a day within the 313 acres of natural splendor is good for the soul. *botgarden.uga.edu, (706) 542-1244*

UNIVERSITY OF GEORGIA, ATHENS

If you live in Georgia, you immediately associate Athens with the flagship university that occupies various locations throughout the city. The University of Georgia is old, so old in fact that it is the first state-chartered university in the United States. The general assembly chartered UGA in 1785, which would eventually be located on 633-acres on the banks of the Oconee River in Athens. Conveniently, one of the most beautiful and historic parts of the campus flows right into the downtown area, providing visitors with easy access to

The Arch is an icon on the UGA campus.

the manicured grounds and stunning architecture. Crossing Broad Street and passing by (not through) the small but iconic Arch (students know not to walk under the structure until the day they graduate) brings you into North Campus, where you find a mix of stately buildings and old oak trees. If you have time, check out the impressive Georgia Museum of Art or attend one of the many athletic events on campus every week. *uga.edu, (706) 542-0842*

📷 SANDY CREEK PARK AND NATURE CENTER, ATHENS

If you feel like getting a bit of exercise with your fresh air, you could do a

Live Music in Athens

If you love live music, Athens is your place. Acts big and small roll through the downtown area almost nightly, and the intimate venues provide a stark, and often welcome, contrast to the much larger offerings in major cities. There is rarely a bad seat in the house, allowing you to get up close and personal with musicians spanning all genres. While the **Georgia Theatre** (georgiatheatre.com, 706-850-7670) and **40 Watt** (40watt.com, 706-549-7871) are the most well-known locations (and for good reason), you'll find a large offering of live music almost every night of the week. Pick up a free copy of the venerable *Flagpole* (flagpole.com, 706-549-9523) for an always up-to-date calendar of events.

The rooftop of the Georgia Theatre is a popular spot for a drink and a bite to eat.

lot worse than Sandy Creek, located just north of downtown. Part education, part recreation, this park offers exhibits and several hiking trails. Sandy Creek is actually comprised of two locations, separated by the four-mile Cook's Trail that winds its way through the surrounding wetlands. You can make the hike between the two, or do things the old-fashioned way and get in your car. Sandy Creek has a large lake (complete with beach), canoes and kayaks, Frisbee golf, multi-sport fields, and plenty to explore. The nature center is completely free while the park charges a small entrance fee. Both are closed on Monday. *athensclarkecounty*

.com/sandycreeknaturecenter, (706) 613-3615

AVID BOOKSHOP, ATHENS

With the rise of Amazon and the struggles of even the largest national booksellers, Avid is a breath of fresh air in the literary world. This local, independent bookstore has found a successful formula that has established a loyal following in the Athens area. The shelves are stocked full of books that appeal to even the pickiest reader, and much of the store is curated by the booklovers who work there. Handwritten notes and short reviews adorn the shelves, helping patrons discover new writers or venture outside of their comfort zones. *avidbookshop.com, (706) 352-2060*

CINE, ATHENS

In the days of megaplexes and IMAX screens, Cine provides a more personal and intimate movie-going experience. It is so beloved by residents in Athens that hundreds of citizens donated money to help purchase the building in which it resides, staving off a possible eviction. Cheap popcorn, reasonable drinks, and a variety of films you don't usually find in your larger theatres all contribute to a memorable night at the movies. *athenscine.com, (706) 353-3343*

BEAR HOLLOW ZOO, ATHENS

Right in the middle of Athens you can find a zoo, lake, playground, and a bit of hiking as well. The zoo is home to a variety of rescued animals (native to Georgia) that can no longer survive in the wild. Explore their natural habitat from elevated walkways that wind throughout the park. Afterward, venture down to the lake and playground, or go for a hike on the peaceful Birchmore Trail. *athensclarkecounty .com/2757/Bear-Hollow-Zoo; (706) 613-3580.*

BLUE WILLOW INN RESTAURANT, SOCIAL CIRCLE

Want to step back in time and have a mouth-watering Southern meal in a historic house? Then look no farther than this Greek Revival mansion located a short walk from downtown.

Cine is a breath of fresh air in the age of huge multiplexes.

Dining in Athens

If you are a foodie, you will find much to like throughout Athens. No matter where you are located inside the perimeter (the highway that encircles the city) you are a short drive from a highly satisfying meal. Athens is divided into quite a few neighborhoods, and perhaps the most exclusive is Five Points, centered around the intersection of Milledge and Lumpkin streets. From the laid back, fresh Latin American food of **Cali and Tito's** (make sure to order a side of Yuca Frita) to Hugh Acheson's award-winning flagship restaurant **5&10** (fiveandten.com, 706-546-7300), your taste buds have much to look forward to. You might also check out the mouth-watering menu at **Donna Chang's** (donnachang's.com, 706-215-9100), an upscale Chinese restaurant with highly refined takes on your favorite classics. Make sure to save room for their delectable homemade ice cream.

Craving even more selection? Head into downtown where you will find a seemingly unending assortment of restaurants and bars. **South Kitchen and Bar** (southkitchenbar .com, 706-395-6125) offers a modern take on Southern classics, as does **The Place** (the-placeathens.com, 706-850-2988). If you are craving some authentic Thai, then check out the unassuming **Thai Spoon** (thaispoonathens.com, 706-548-9222) and their extensive menu. For upscale dining you can't beat **The National** (thenationalrestaurant.com, 706-549-3450), this European-inspired establishment is located directly across the street from Creature Comforts brewery (highlighted in the craft beer section). Speaking of beer, if you are a connoisseur then **Trappeze** (trappezepub.com, 706-543-8997) should be a must-visit, with almost 30 beers on draught and hundreds more in bottles. Oh, and the food is quite good as well.

There are plenty of locations throughout Athens to quell your appetite.

Dine on Southern staples such as chicken and dumplings and fried green tomatoes, then relax on the stately front porch, complete with large white columns often found on the most impressive antebellum homes. Open for lunch and dinner Wednesday through Sunday. Call ahead for reservations. *bluewillowinn.com*, *(770) 464-2131*

MONASTERY OF THE HOLY SPIRIT, CONYERS

Peace, tranquility, and beautiful architecture are hallmarks of this immense 2,300-acre estate to the east of Atlanta. Open daily to the general public, the monastery offers a harmonious blend of nature along with the impressive display of structural design that began over 70 years ago. A museum, kid-friendly exhibits, bonsai trees, beautiful stained glass, and even a café on the property all contribute to a relaxing destination for visitors from all over the world. If the weather is nice, make sure to wear comfortable shoes so you can enjoy the nature trail that meanders through the property. *trappist.net*, *(770) 483-8705*

◻ HARD LABOR CREEK STATE PARK, RUTLEDGE

For outdoor lovers, this 5,800-acre park has a little bit of everything. A beautiful cascading creek winds its way through the rolling terrain, giving life to the stately hardwoods and variety of woodland creatures that are native to the area. Play a round of golf (regular or mini), hike some trails, explore the region by bicycle, or enjoy the picturesque lake, which offers a beach, kayaks, canoes, and paddleboats. If you want a bite to eat, make the short drive over to Rutledge and grab a sandwich from **The Caboose** (thecabookseinrutledge.com, 706-557-9021), a renovated train car on the downtown square. *gastateparks.org/HardLaborCreek*, *706-557-3001*

MADISON

There's a reason why this small town has received numerous national awards. If there is a quintessential Southern town in Georgia, this is it. With plenty of shopping and dining in the downtown area, along with beautifully preserved antebellum homes throughout the city, the Southern charm is thick and authentic. Grab

The tranquillity of the monastery brings visitors from Georgia and beyond.

Antebellum homes are seemingly everywhere in the town of Madison.

a bite to eat at the **Madison Chophouse Grille** (madisonchophouse .com, 706-342-9009) after you have strolled the square and perused the range of locally-owned antique stores and gift shops. If you love fine chocolate, look no further than **Antique Sweets** (antiquesweets.com, 706-342-0034). Chances are, when you start to explore this charming town you will want to get a better look at the stunning architecture, so the **Madison-Morgan Cultural Center** (mmcc-arts.org, 706-342-4743) and the **Rogers House** (706-343-0190) are both worth a visit. *visitmadisonga .com, (706) 342-4454*

Sherman's March

The final two months of the year 1864 were not kind to the state of Georgia, especially along a 285-mile route from Atlanta to Savannah. It was then that General William T. Sherman put a punctuation mark on the North's pending victory in the Civil War. Two groups of soldiers, totaling nearly 60,000, started a march from Atlanta down to Savannah, with the groups taking slightly different routes to impart as much chaos as possible on the Georgia countryside. The march was met with little resistance from the dwindling Confederate soldiers, and while many a farm and bridge were burned across Georgia, fortunately most of the towns and cities remained intact. You can see this with your own eyes as you pass through towns such as Madison, Eatonton, Milledgeville, and Savannah; you will be treated to beautiful antebellum homes that withstood the bloodiest war in the history of the nation. The psychological impact of this march cannot be understated, as the civilians quickly realized that their property could no longer be protected by the Confederate Army. It marked a crucial turning point in the Civil War, which officially ended five months later.

Sherman's March to the Sea was one of the most pivotal moments in the Civil War.

Hiking trails and serenity await visitors to the remote Watson Mill Bridge State Park.

📷 🌳 WATSON MILL BRIDGE STATE PARK, COMER

The centerpiece of this park is the working covered bridge that spans the South Fork River. A small waterfall is located under the span of the bridge, creating a picturesque setting ideal for a picnic or leisurely stroll. There are hiking trails on both sides of the river, with one leading to the remnants of an old mill and hydroelectric plant. If you like to get away from it all (this park is many miles from the nearest small town), this adventure is well worth your time. *gastateparks.org/watsonmillbridge*, (706) 783-5349

📷 ELDER MILL COVERED BRIDGE, WATKINSVILLE

There aren't a whole lot of covered bridges left in Georgia, especially ones you can actually drive across. Thanks to a dedicated group of

Elder Mill Covered Bridge is one of the few covered bridges still in service today.

A Horse of Iron

Every state has its roadside oddities, and Georgia is no different. Although to call this an oddity might be doing it a disservice, because it represents art, history, and a great deal of pride for University of Georgia students and alumni. Back in 1954, world-renowned artist Abbott Pattison from the Chicago Institute of Art created this 4,000-pound sculpture to be placed on the UGA campus, but it was met with criticism and vandalism. After students attempted to light the statue on fire, it was determined to be too problematic to keep on campus and was stored in a secret location for years before it was put out to pasture on a farm south of Athens. Perhaps the saying about time healing all wounds is true, because the statue is now a beloved part of the university's lore and is visited daily by students, alumni, and curious travelers who pass the field on Georgia Highway 15, around 12 miles south of Watkinsville. A small parking area and path allows access to the statue, which is surrounded by rolling farmland and the nearby Oconee River.

The Iron Horse is an icon for the University of Georgia, even though it sits in the middle of a field.

residents, the Elder Mill Covered Bridge was preserved and moved to its current location in 1924, where it has remained in use ever since. Nestled in a small valley between two steep hills, the bridge accommodates local traffic every day, and the cascading Rose Creek that flows underneath contributes to the serenity of the location.

The Robert Toombs House offers plenty of history within the museum.

WASHINGTON

For history buffs, a trip to Washington is well worth the time. Situated halfway between Athens and Augusta, it is a perfect stopping point between the two cities. Several wonderfully preserved buildings from the turn of the seventeenth century are as beautiful as they are educational. The Mary Willis Library, Washington Historical Museum, and Robert Toombs House all showcase historical artifacts, and you can get some fresh country air by exploring the nearby Kettle Creek Revolutionary Battlefield. *washingtonwilkes.org, (706) 678-2013*

A.H. STEPHENS STATE PARK, CRAWFORDVILLE

Just down the road from Washington is another location steeped in history. This state park offers some nice outdoor opportunities, but the centerpiece is the Confederate Museum and neighboring Liberty Hall, home of the vice president of the Confederacy, A.H. Stephens. Visitors are treated to a fully renovated home, faithful to its late-nineteenth-century construction. The museum is full of Civil War artifacts, including weapons, documents, and clothing. *gastateparks.org/ah stephens, (706) 456-2602*

Festivals

There are plenty of festivals all over the Peach State each and every year, from bicycle races to concerts, from wine to cherry blossoms. Almost any given weekend has events throughout the state. These are a few of the highlights.

International Cherry Blossom Festival, Macon

Every March, thousands of visitors from all over the world descend on Macon to soak up the beautiful cherry blossoms budding on the 350,000 Yoshino cherry trees across the city. While the blooms begin in mid-March, the end of the month they are at their peak, creating a landscape of bright white blossoms and faint almond fragrance. The trees throughout Macon can be sourced back to a realtor in 1949 who owned a single cherry tree in his backyard. Its striking beauty eventually led to a community-wide effort to plant the fast-growing trees throughout the city, which led to the first festival in 1982. The festival brings in music, food, amusements, tours of historical parts of the city, and much more. It is celebrated as one of the top festivals in the United States. *cherryblossom.com, (478) 330-7050*

Oktoberfest, Helen

While the original Oktoberfest in Germany might last a bit over two weeks, Helen figures that is way too short for a celebration. Instead, the city breaks the festival down into weekend celebrations that begin in early September and then transition into daily affairs for the month of October. German-style bands pour into town, providing plenty of music and entertainment for the visitors who wander the streets and pour into (pun intended) bars in search of beer and revelry. The massive Helen Festhalle hosts the event, although celebrations can be found all over town, along with bratwurst and Reuben sandwiches. Located in the foothills of the Appalachian Mountains, the area offers plenty of outdoor activities to satisfy those who need a little break from the merriment. *helenchamber.com/oktoberfest.html, (706) 878-1908*

The Cherry Blossom Festival in Macon is one of the largest in the southeast.

Georgia Apple Festival, Ellijay

For two weekends in the fall, this small mountain town is the epicenter for everything apple. The cooler temps and higher elevations of the north Georgia mountains create a perfect environment for growing apple trees, with more than 10 varieties that thrive in the state. The festival itself offers 300 vendors bringing arts and crafts, food, music, and more to the area. A parade and antique car show also provide plenty to watch during your time in the area. Of course, if you drive up to the mountains then you should pick some of your own apples from the more than 10 nearby orchards. *georgiaapplefestival.org,* (706) 636-4500

Atlanta Food and Wine Festival, Atlanta

A foodies' delight, this annual festival at the beginning of June brings in some of the top chefs from the United States and beyond to showcase their skills for the thousands of attendees. There are so many different tickets and experiences to choose from, it will take a lot of time, and budgetary restraint, to make your choices.

The Festhalle is the epicenter of Oktoberfest in Helen.

Pick your own apples at one of many orchards near Ellijay.

The historic district on Jekyll Island is a pristine setting for the Shrimp and Grits festival.

Heart-pounding racing is a hallmark of this annual race through the streets of Athens.

Learning experiences, a tasting tent, lunches, dinners, and so much more are available, giving you unparalleled access to some of the most talented chefs, mixologists, distillers, authors, and sommeliers in the food and wine industry. *atlfoodandwinefestival.com, (404) 474-7330*

Shrimp and Grits Festival, Jekyll Island

Held in the fall every year, this festival celebrates one of the biggest fishing exports for the state of Georgia. Food, an artists' market, kids' zone, and live music are just some of the offerings for visitors who venture over to this barrier island. The stately buildings, majestic oaks, and pristine lawn found throughout the historic district create a perfect setting for enjoying this Southern delicacy. A craft beer festival is also held at the same time, ensuring the opportunity to wash down the fresh shrimp and grits with a delicious beer. *jekyllisland.com*

Twilight Criterium, Athens

A signature bicycle race that has been going on for more than 40 years helps bring downtown Athens alive at the end of April. A weekend of music, kids' activities, and bicycle-related events all lead up to the main event on Saturday night: 50 miles of racing on a one-kilometer course that runs through downtown amidst a throng of spectators. Professionals from around the world participate in the race, ensuring an exciting (and fast) event that has everyone's hearts racing. Afterward, you can celebrate at one (or more) of the plentiful bars in the downtown area. In fact, the city leads the nation in bars per square mile, with more than 80 in downtown alone. *athenstwilight.com*

Georgia Peach Festival, Peach County

It's only natural to have a festival that honors the Peach State, and that festival, of course, occurs in Peach County. Thousands of visitors arrive in June to celebrate the delectable fruit that is exported by the bushel (1.7 million to be exact) every year in Georgia. The festival features plenty of food, arts, and crafts, but perhaps the most significant event is the baking and tasting of the world's largest peach cobbler. Stretching 11-feet long and 5-feet wide, the cobbler contains 90 pounds of butter, 150 pounds of sugar, 150 pounds of flour, 32 gallons of milk, and 75 gallons of peaches. The result is an eye-popping cobbler that attendees line up to taste, and for good reason. *gapeachfestival.com, (478) 825-4002*

This might be the only time Atlanta's traffic is beautiful.

ATLANTA

The cultural epicenter of the entire state sits in the northern Piedmont, with rolling hills and an occasional mountain rising out of a landscape inhabited by more than 5.9 million people in the metropolitan area. The actual city of Atlanta is much smaller, with roughly 500,000 citizens residing within the city limits. These people live "inside the Perimeter," a colloquial term that references the massive Interstate 285 that is 12 lanes wide in some places and handles more than 250,000 cars per day. While the metro area includes a wide range of towns, cities, and bedroom communities where housing is more affordable, inside that loop is where you find a metropolis rich with history, culture, culinary excellence, and vibrant nightlife. It's not a bad idea to just start downtown and slowly work your way out, exploring more and experiencing all that the ATL has to offer.

Atlanta has had several names over the years, starting with the Terminus, evolving to Marthasville, and finally becoming Atlanta. Of course, modern times have brought about even more colloquial names for this metropolis, including the ATL, A-Town, and The Empire City of the South. No matter what you call it, you'll find that it is a melting pot of ever-evolving culture that offers so much that practically anyone can find a place to feel included and welcome. Perhaps this is why it continues to be one of the fastest-growing metro areas in the country.

You can trace the city's roots back to the early 1800s when a railroad station connected travelers from Tennessee to parts across

The Atlanta skyline is dramatic and ever-changing.

Visitors will still find traces of the Olympics that were held in Atlanta in 1996.

Atlanta's roots can be traced back to the railroad station that was constructed in the early 1800s.

An eerie glow in the sky over Atlanta is the result of summer storms.

Georgia. A small city emerged and began to grow, fueled by travel and the potential for commerce due to the railroad and nearby Chattahoochee River. Unfortunately for the city, this main railroad hub became an easy target during the Civil War, and much of the city was destroyed by General Sherman and his Union soldiers as the war came to a close. Ironically, this actually helped Atlanta become what it is today, because the federal occupation established it as a Military District, and the capital of Georgia was soon moved from Milledgeville to Atlanta.

Since then, it seems as if Atlanta has been constantly accelerating in growth and is now one of the largest transportation hubs in the world. Between the air traffic and the intersection of Interstates 20, 85, and 75, there are few people or products that don't eventually pass through this booming metropolis. You've probably heard almost legendary stories about the traffic in this city, and many of them are likely true. Don't expect to go anywhere fast during the morning and afternoon rush hours. Plan your days accordingly and things will be far less stressful. The good news is that there are many, many places in the city accessible by foot or bicycle, eliminating the need for those noisy engines that fill the streets throughout the day. You could spend several days in the city, seeing many of the essential attractions, all without needing a car. There are so many places to enjoy and experience that they cannot all be included here, but we will look at some of the highlights from around the metro area. *atlanta.net, (404) 521-6600*

Libations in Atlanta

Alpharetta

Cherry Street Halcyon
cherrystreetbrewing.com

Currahee Brewing
curraheebrew.com

Jekyll Brewing
jekyllbrewing.com

Atlanta

Atlanta Brewing Co.
redbrickbrewing.com

Atlanta Hard Cider Co.
atlantahardcider.com

Best End Brewing
bestendbrewing.com

Bold Monk Brewing
boldmonkbrewingco.com

Eventide Brewing
eventidebrewing.com

Fire Maker Brewing Company
firemakerbeer.com

Gordon Biersch—Buckhead
gordonbiersch.com

Halfway Crooks Beer
halfwaycrooks.beer

Khonso Brewing
khonsobrewing.com

Max Lagers
maxlagers.com

Monday Night Brewing and
Monday Night Garage
mondaynightbrewing.com

New Realm Brewing Co.
newrealmbrewing.com

Orpheus Brewing
orpheusbrewing.com

Park Tavern
parktavern.com

Scofflaw Brewing Co.
scofflawbeer.com

Second Self Brewing
secondselfbeer.com

STATS Brewpub
statsatl.com

Steady Hand Beer Co.
steadyhandbeer.com

Sweetwater Brewery
sweetwaterbrew.com

Torched Hop Brewpub
torchedhopbrewing.com

Terrapin Taproom
terrapintaproom.com

Urban Tree Cidery
urbantreecidery.com

Wild Heaven West End
wildheavenbeer.com/west-end

Wrecking Bar
wreckingbarbrewpub.com

Avondale Estates

Lost Druid Brewing Company
thelostdruid.com

Wild Heaven
wildheavencraftbeers.com

Braselton

Chateau Elan Winery
chateauelan.com

Canton

Green Line Brewing Co.
greenlinebrews.com

Reformation Brewery
reformationbrewery.com/canton

Chamblee

Contrast Artisan Ales
contrastartisanales.com

Hopstix
hopstixbrewing.com

Cumming

Cherry Street Brewing
cherrystreetbrewing.com

NoFo Brewing Company
nofobrew.co

There are seemingly endless breweries throughout the Atlanta metro area.

Decatur
Blue Tarp
bluetarpbrew.com

Sceptre Brewing Arts
sceptrebrewingarts.com

Three Taverns
threetavernsbrewery.com

Twain's
twains.net

Duluth
Good Word Brewing & Public House
goodwordbrewing.com

Dunwoody
Porter BBQ & Brewery
porterbbqbrewery.com

Hapeville
Arches Brewing
archesbrewing.com

Johns Creek
Six Bridges Brewing
sixbridgesbrewing.com

Kennesaw
Burnt Hickory Brewery
burnthickorybrewery.com

Dry County Brewing
drycountybrewco.com

Lake City
North 2 South Cider Works
n2sciderworks.com

Lawrenceville
Slow Pour Brewing
slowpourbrewing.com

Marietta
Glover Park Brewery
gloverparkbrewery.com

Ironmonger
naughtysoda.com

Johnnie MacCracken's
johnniemaccrackens.com

Red Hare
redharebrewing.com

Schoolhouse Brewing
schoolhousebeer.com

Shezmu Cellars
shezmcellars.com

Treehorn Cider
treehorncider.com

Powder Springs
Railcat Brewing Company
railcatbrewing.com

Peachtree Corners
Anderby Brewing
anderbybrewing.com

Roswell
From the Earth Brewing Co.
ftebrewing.com

Gate City Brewing Co.
gatecitybrewing.com

Variant Brewing Co.
variantbrewing.com

Sandy Springs
Pontoon Brewing
pontoonbrewing.com

Porter Pizza & Brewery
porterpizzabrewery.com

Stone Mountain
Stone Mountain Brewery
germanrestaurant.com

Sugar Hill
Indio Brewing
indiobrewing.com

Suwanee
Monkey Wrench Brewing Co.
monkeywrenchbrewing.com

Stillfire Brewing
stillfirebrewing.com

Tucker
Tucker Brewing Company
tuckerbrewing.com

High Card Brewing
highcardbrewing.com

Woodstock
Reformation Brewery Downtown
reformationbrewery.com

Reformation Brewery Foundry
reformationbrewery.com

FERNBANK MUSEUM OF NATURAL HISTORY, ATLANTA

A world of dinosaurs, 3D movies, nature quests, and interactive exhibits are just a few of the compelling attractions at this museum. When you first enter you are greeted by the Giants of the Mesozoic, featuring the largest dinosaur ever classified. The impressive display provides a sense of just how large these beasts were. If the weather cooperates, you can explore the interpretive trails in the surrounding forest, walking high above the ground on elevated walkways that weave through the trees. After exploring the almost 2 miles of pathways steeped with interpretive exhibits, head back inside to check out the many permanent collections as well as catch a giant-screen 3D movie. *fernbankmuseum.org, (404) 929-6300*

DID YOU KNOW? The Atlanta CityPass is a cost-efficient way to experience many of Atlanta's most popular offerings at a discounted rate. The pass is good for 9 days and gives you access to a large variety of locations. *citypass.com, (208) 787-4300*

The Fernbank Museum of Natural History will impress almost anyone who walks through the doors.

WORLD OF COCA-COLA, ATLANTA

One of the most popular attractions in Atlanta exists for a reason—the world's love affair with the syrupy goodness invented by a pharmacist in the late 1800s. His formula opened the door to a multi-billion-dollar soft drink empire, literally creating an industry that had never existed before. As the drink became more popular, competitors popped up with their own products, muddying the market. Along came Coke's unique glass bottle, an iconic design that has evolved over the years but is still distinctly Coke. Visitors to this sprawling complex—just a short distance from the world headquarters of the company—learn all about the drink, its role in pop culture, how it is bottled, and how it tastes all over the world. There are 60 different flavors available for you to sample, so prepare your taste buds. *worldofcoca-cola .com, (404) 676-5151*

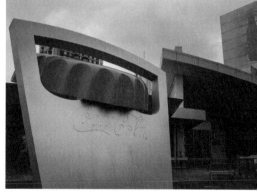

Sweet syrup and carbonated water took the world by storm when Coca-Cola was invented.

CNN CENTER, ATLANTA

A tour of the studios at CNN offer a behind-the-scenes look at how one of the largest news organizations in the world is run. Guides explain everything that goes into an international broadcast. The center sits in the middle of downtown, offering a variety of

One of the biggest news companies in the world is headquartered in Atlanta.

dining and shopping options. *center .cnn.com, (404) 827-2300*

GEORGIA AQUARIUM, ATLANTA

Many cities around the world have aquariums, but few come close to the one in Atlanta. Second largest in the world, this aquarium offers an almost unmatched up close and personal experience with marine life that inhabit streams, rivers, and oceans all over the globe. From the $110

million dolphin exhibit that features live shows several times per day, to a 6.3-million-gallon tank that hosts four whale sharks along with more than 50 other species. Watching these animals swim and interact can be very calming, and a long tunnel that runs underneath the main tank puts you at the bottom of a manmade ocean where you can observe the fascinating interplay of the ecosystem. The aquarium is enormous and offers a wide range of exhibits, bringing in visitors from near and far. It gets crowded, but if you can visit on a weekday you might not have to share the space quite as much. *georgia aquarium.org, (404) 581-4000*

ZOO ATLANTA, ATLANTA

Education, conservation, and up-close observation are the hallmarks of this 40-acre property located within Grant Park. The zoo opened in 1889 after a traveling show ran out of money and left the animals in Atlanta, where they were eventually auctioned off to a businessman

Colorful pink flamingoes greet visitors who walk through the gates of Zoo Atlanta.

About Those Peaches

It's hard to travel far in Georgia without seeing the word "peach." In fact, the Atlanta metro area alone has more than 70 roads with that word in them, which caused plenty of wrong turns and frustration for drivers before the days of Google Maps. Interestingly, though this ubiquitous fruit grows throughout central and south Georgia, peaches originally hail from China. It wasn't until the late 1800s that they started being grown for agricultural purposes here in the United States. Georgia peaches can be traced back to the tiny town of Marshallville, located a short drive from Perry. It was here that the first seeds were planted, resulting in some very tasty peaches about five years later. After a small bug named the Boll Weevil came in and decimated the cotton production in the South, Georgia had a big agricultural hole to fill. Production of peaches was ramped up and eventually the nickname "The Peach State" was used to promote this new cash crop that was proliferating throughout the state. While many point out that Georgia ranks third in the United States in total peach production, the farmers here still believe the best tasting peaches come out of Georgia soil.

It's hard to go far without seeing Georgia Peaches, especially throughout the summer.

and donated to the city. This planted the seed of what would eventually become a flourishing space that houses giant pandas, gorillas, giraffes, and more than 1,300 other animals. Visitors have access to a variety of animal exhibits, as well as a plant exhibit, a petting zoo, and multiple playgrounds. After you leave the zoo, take the opportunity to explore the surrounding Grant Park. *zooatlanta.org, (404) 624-9453*

NATIONAL CENTER FOR CIVIL AND HUMAN RIGHTS, ATLANTA

It makes perfect sense that the city where Martin Luther King Jr. was born should house a museum that champions many of the ideals he stood for. The central focus of this museum is to honor the accomplishments of the many individuals who have fought for equal human rights all over the world. Located in the center of downtown Atlanta, the facility offers a mix of temporary and permanent exhibits that highlight worldwide human rights movements, past and present. The goal is for visitors to experience the issues and have a greater understanding of the challenges that marginalized people have faced and continue to face. Arrive with some curiosity and you are bound to leave inspired. *civilandhumanrights.org, (678) 999-8990*

COLLEGE FOOTBALL HALL OF FAME, ATLANTA

If you love football, and you not only want to learn more about it but actually experience it, then this stop is well worth your time. Visitors can explore the 95,000-square-foot facility and participate in a wide range

Helmets from every college football team adorn the wall of the Hall of Fame.

of interactive exhibits, testing their skills and knowledge of the most popular sport in the United States. Not only will you learn about the best players to ever suit up at the college level, but you get some exercise on the indoor playing field, including the chance to kick a field goal and gain some appreciation for the talent required to send one through the uprights. *cfbhall.com, (404) 880-4800*

CENTENNIAL OLYMPIC PARK, ATLANTA

This centrally located park opened in 1996, just in time for the Summer Olympics in Atlanta. It now serves as an educational destination where visitors learn about the Olympic Games as well as the city of Atlanta. An hour-long, self-guided walking loop takes visitors throughout the 22-acre park, with an audio narration that can be downloaded to any smartphone. Make sure you stop by the fountains, with cascading water that erupts from the Olympic rings embedded in the ground. After the tour, walk over to the **SkyView Ferris wheel** for unobstructed views throughout downtown Atlanta. The 180-foot high structure rotates four times, with visitors sitting in air-conditioned gondolas that provide welcome relief from the summer heat of Georgia. *gwcca .org/centennial-olympic-park, (404) 223-4000*

MARTIN LUTHER KING JR. NATIONAL HISTORICAL PARK, ATLANTA

There are few individuals in the history of the United States who singlehandedly transformed culture and society like Martin Luther King Jr. did. Visitors to this park, which actually consists of several buildings in the Atlanta area, gain a greater

Gone But Not Forgotten

Born and raised in Atlanta, novelist Margaret Mitchell (Margaret Munnerlyn Mitchell Marsh to be exact) experienced times of success and uncertainty during the early twentieth century. She was a natural writer, crafting her own stories and books at a very early age. Mitchell left for Smith College in Massachusetts but had to return after her mother died of influenza, eventually taking a job with the *Atlanta Journal* that provided her with a steady outlet for her writing. A broken ankle eventually led to her quitting her job at the paper, but her need to write was unyielding so she recalled the stories she was told as a young woman and began a novel about the Civil War and Reconstruction. Little did she know, the disjointed manuscript she worked on for over nine years would lead to the creation of one of the greatest American novels of all time. When *Gone with the Wind* was finally published in 1936, it went on to sell more copies than any other novel in US publishing history and would lead to Mitchell earning the Pulitzer Prize in 1937. All of this brought the author lots of attention—more than she desired. She tried to stay under the radar, serving with the Red Cross during World War II and then, in 1949, she was tragically struck and killed by a passing car on Peachtree Street in downtown Atlanta. Her memory lives on to this day, in part because of the **Margaret Mitchell House** which sits in the middle of Midtown. Here visitors can walk through a museum and the apartment where Mitchell penned her masterpiece. *atlantahistorycenter.com*, **(404) 814-4000**

The Margaret Mitchell House stands in stark contrast to the modern skyscrapers in downtown Atlanta.

Centennial Park anchors downtown Atlanta, providing greenspace and event space for residents and visitors.

Fountains provide cool relief for visitors in the hot summer months.

understanding of King's formative years, and learn extensively about his life and contributions. The park includes his boyhood home, Ebenezer Baptist Church (where he and his dad were both pastors), as well as his gravesite. Prepare to be moved as you learn so much more about this icon of the twentieth century. *nps.gov/malu, (404) 331-5190*

HIGH MUSEUM OF ART, ATLANTA

The striking modern design and constantly changing exhibitions help make this museum one of the best in the southeast. The permanent collection contains more than 15,000 thousand works that fill the extensive and airy space, including African Art, photography, sculptures, and a selection of creations from artists around Atlanta. A newly installed family learning gallery allows budding artists of all ages to enjoy the world of art through a variety of hands-on activities. New exhibitions arrive throughout the year, so check the website for the latest information. *high.org, (404) 733-4400*

OAKLAND CEMETERY, ATLANTA

If the weather is good and you want to get some exercise somewhere quiet, peaceful, and free of massive crowds, then you can't do much better than this location just outside of downtown. The final resting place of some of the most influential people in Georgia, this cemetery was established in 1850. Originally six acres, it swelled to 48 acres after the Civil War, with many of the gravesites occupied by soldiers. Notable residents include golfing legend Bobby Jones and *Gone with the Wind* author Margaret Mitchell, who won the Pulitzer Prize in 1937. Even if you aren't interested in reading the headstones, a walk through the beautiful

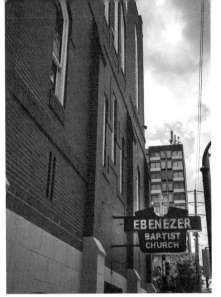

Ebenezer Baptist Church was a cornerstone for Martin Luther King Jr.

A variety of art and modern architecture are hallmarks of the High Museum.

Lots of history within a peaceful setting, Oakland Cemetery is a popular place to enjoy some peace and quiet.

gardens of this cemetery will conjure up a sense of appreciation for the world in which we live, as well as how fleeting it can be. *oaklandcemetery .com, (404) 688-2107*

JIMMY CARTER PRESIDENTIAL LIBRARY AND MUSEUM, ATLANTA

Georgia has only produced one US president, so this library and museum is certainly one-of-a-kind in the Peach State. The 39th president, Jimmy Carter, served from 1977 until 1981. When he left office the planning began for his library in Atlanta. The impressive facility is 70,000 square-feet in size and houses a museum dedicated to his life, as well as an extensive archive of records related to his administration. The museum includes plenty of insight into what it is like to serve as the President of the United States, including an accurately modeled Oval Office. *jimmycarter library.gov, (404) 865-7100*

SWAN HOUSE, ATLANTA

Make no mistake about it, even though Atlanta is a cosmopolitan city full of skyscrapers, modern architecture, and residents hailing from all parts of the globe, it is still steeped in Southern tradition. The Swan House at the Atlanta History Center is a shining architectural example of the Second Renaissance Revival. The home and surroundings are immaculate, with lush landscaping and huge columns that project wealth and stature to everyone who visits. Built by an affluent couple in the 1920s, the home was immaculately restored in 2004 and contains many furnishings original to the 1920s and '30s. *atlanta historycenter.com, (404) 814-4000*

POLARIS, ATLANTA

On top of the Hyatt Regency in the heart of downtown Atlanta sits an icon that first opened its doors in 1967. This rotating restaurant has an

The Jimmy Carter Presidential Library and Museum offers a wealth of information about Georgia's only president.

The gorgeous architecture of the Swan House is a treat for visitors.

The rotating Polaris offers fine dining with a spectacular view.

Atlanta Nightlife

A cosmopolitan city of this size is bound to have a whole host of places to go after the sun sets, and an entire book could be dedicated to the myriad bars and nightclubs that can be found throughout the metro area. Here are just a few highlights to provide some options for almost anyone looking for some entertainment.

The Painted Duck (thepaintedduckatl .com, 404-352-0048) offers an assortment of drinks and a highly entertaining place in which to consume them. The unique 26,000-square-foot building houses old-school games that set the stage for a night of merriment, including obscure offerings such as duckpin bowling, snookball, and knuckleball. For those wanting something a little more familiar, there is also shuffleboard, air hockey, basketball, and horseshoes.

If dancing is more your thing, check out **Opera** (operaatlanta.com) located in Midtown. It is a place to see and be seen, and the line (and prices) reflect it. For even the most seasoned clubber, the stage and sound system is worth every minute spent standing outside waiting to get in.

On the opposite end of the spectrum is the Atlanta staple **Johnny's Hideaway** (johnnyshideaway.com, 404-233-8026), a dance club with a very different soundtrack. With plenty of retro hits (including Sinatra and Elvis) playing, this dance floor can get crowded, but you are just as likely to see retirees cutting a rug as you are a group of trendy college students.

Of course, packed dance floors aren't for everyone, and there are plenty of dive bars that can provide a bit more of a relaxed evening. When you walk into the iconic **Smith's Old Bar** (smithsoldebar.com, 404-875-1522) you'll be treated to live music, good food, and a laid-back atmosphere. A mix of bands and DJs take the stage throughout the week, ensuring there is always something to listen to as you sip your libation.

You'll hear the live music before you even open the door at the Northside Tavern near downtown Atlanta.

For those who love the blues, the **Northside Tavern** (northsidetavern.com, 404-874-8745) should be on your short list of plans for the evening. Open since the '70s, this place features live blues seven days a week along with an authentic atmosphere that only comes with an establishment that has been around for this long.

An intimate comedy club that brings in big name comics is a perfect recipe for a night filled with laughter, and the famous burger spot next door can conveniently satisfy any hunger you might have. The **Laughing Skull Lounge** (laughingskulllounge .com, 404-369-1017) offers stand-up comedy almost every night of the week, and with only 74 seats you'll be sure to have a great view of the stage. Before or after the show, grab a burger and a brew at **The Vortex** (thevortexatl.com, 404-875-1667). If you are the type who likes to tackle an eating challenge, then the Quadruple Coronary Bypass will test every ounce of your resolve. More than 9,500 calories of burger goodness await, and only two people have ever completed the challenge. Do you have it in you?

New Realm Brewing is a large brewery with plenty of food options located directly on the BeltLine, fueling the masses while providing expansive views of the downtown skyline. Sizable outdoor seating areas on the first and second floors help offset any wait at this popular establishment. Get your palette tingling with the Hoptropolis IPA and then calm things down with the fantastic B-ATL Grilled Cheese. *newrealmbrewing.com, (404) 968-2777*

If you aren't as concerned about craft beer and have a soft spot for beautifully designed industrial space, then **Two Urban Licks** next door to New Realm Brewing is just for you. On a nice day, the massive glass doors roll up to the ceiling, creating an open-air restaurant that serves up meat, fish, and lots of fresh bread. An extensive wine menu and some of the best desserts you will ever put in your mouth round out a memorable dining experience in the Old Fourth Ward neighborhood of Atlanta. *twourbanlicks.com, (404) 522-4622*

The renovation of **Ponce City Market**, a 2.1-million-square-foot building originally used by Sears for the better part of a decade, is a masterclass of thoughtful design and exceptional preservation. The result is a space so extensive that you can literally spend an entire day here without feeling a desire to leave. The first floor offers a collection of eclectic shops, remarkable restaurants, and a massive

Ponce City Market is massive and offers a little bit for everyone, including plenty of activities on the roof.

Sip on some hops and sample some excellent food as you soak in the view from New Realm Brewing.

The retail is great, but many come to Krog Street Market for the variety of food.

is less than stellar, you can grab a glass of wine and listen to some live music at the nearby **City Winery** (citywinery.com/ atlanta/, 404-946-3791), which is adjacent to the market. *poncecitymarket.com, 404-900-7900*

The wildly popular Monday Night Brewing in Atlanta opened a second location, **Monday Night Garage,** on the southern segment of the Beltline back in 2017, and it was received with open arms and bellies. The facility has a taproom, a large outdoor seating area, and a variety of food trucks to satisfy your hunger. If you like the idea of getting some fresh air, playing some ping-pong, and drinking some meticulously crafted beer from one of the many taps, then this is your place. *mondaynightbrewing.com, (404) 352-7703*

Krog Street Market offers a selection of distinctive restaurants and retail stores throughout its nine-acres located on the eastside of the city. Unlike the massive Ponce City Market, this establishment has a more laid-back vibe with smaller crowds. The market, considered one of the best food halls in the United States, offers 13 dining options along with seven retail shops on site. If you can only eat at one place, make it the **Ticonderoga Club** (ticonderogaclub.com, 404-458-4534), opened by three bartenders who know a thing or two about drinks. Along with the libations you'll find a creative menu of meats and seafood. *krogstreetmarket .com, (770) 434-2400*

food hall that will satisfy the culinary cravings of practically anyone. The middle floors are primarily office and residential space, but the top floor is the *coup de grace*, offering a large amusement park, an outdoor bar, and expansive views of the city. After a day of eating and shopping, head to the roof for a round of mini-golf and a relaxing drink as the vibrant city buzzes ten stories below. If the weather

unmistakable shape, and charm, that is well worth the cost of the excellent mixed drinks and varied seasonal menu. With a slow rotation providing an ever-changing view of the downtown skyline, the restaurant and bar provide a memorable evening as you take in the panoramas from 22 stories

in the air. If you aren't interested in the food, then relax with a drink on one of the cozy sofas while you appreciate the well-executed mix of retro and modern design throughout the interior. *polarisatlanta.com, (404) 460-6425*

STARLIGHT DRIVE-IN MOVIE THEATRE, ATLANTA

Not interested in clubs or late nights at the bar? Are there kids in your family who have no concept of what a drive-in movie theater is all about? Chances are, spending an evening enjoying a few movies at the only remaining drive-in theater in Atlanta will be a fun experience and lead to wonderful memories. The Starlight opened in 1949 and has been in business ever since. It now serves as a throwback to yesteryear, when old Ford Fairlanes and Chevy Corvairs rumbled down the road and into the parking lot for an evening of family-friendly entertainment. Show up before dark and grab a spot near the screen before tuning your FM radio to pick up the broadcast of the double feature. A snack bar is onsite for all your movie-watching delicacies, but the nostalgia you'll feel costs nothing at all. *starlightdrivein.com, (404) 627-5786*

TINY DOORS, ATLANTA

If you are looking for an easy excuse to explore parts of Atlanta that you otherwise would never even know about, then the Tiny Doors art

There are tiny doors all over the city, providing visitors with a reason to get off the beaten path.

project is just the ticket. Installation art pieces have popped up all over Atlanta, bringing a sense of aesthetics, wonder, and a hint of adventure to the locals and tourists who have explored their locations. These seven-inch-tall doors have been placed throughout the city, each with a unique design that faithfully represents the neighborhood in which they are located. The website has an interactive map that you can use to locate the doors, giving you the chance to explore some of the lesser-known parts of the city while appreciating a tiny, yet vibrant and creative part of the Atlanta art scene. *tiny doorsatl.com*

MARY MAC'S TEA ROOM, ATLANTA

If you asked locals where is the one place everyone should eat when they visit Atlanta, you will certainly hear this venerable and historic restaurant mentioned often. Since its opening in 1945, workers have made everything from scratch each morning, including all the breads and desserts. This is Southern dining at its best, with fried chicken, fried green tomatoes, and incredible cinnamon buns that will have you salivating. One of the local favorites is the sweet potato soufflé, but the menu is so extensive that it's difficult to make a decision. Open seven days a week, it is well worth a trip if you want to dine on exemplary Southern cuisine. *marymacs.com, (404) 876-1800*

THE BELTLINE

The Atlanta BeltLine is a new and ever-evolving multi-use path that passes through neighborhoods, parks, and various boroughs as it winds around Atlanta. Construction is ongoing, but the final result will be 33 miles of trails, 1,300 acres of

Piedmont Park 📷 🌳

On a beautiful day, expect to find thousands of people enjoying the great outdoors in this 180-acre expanse of trees, lakes, fields, and so much more. The park dates back to the early 1800s when it was nothing more than a serene forest. A settler purchased the land for a modest sum and transformed it into farmland and built a cabin. Back then, Atlanta was in its infancy, but its perpetual growth resulted in the repurposing of the land to host traveling expositions and fairs. It wasn't until 1904 that the city purchased the privately held park and opened it as an amenity to the many residents who had relocated to the area.

Today the park is a thriving space enjoyed by residents and visitors alike, paralleling bustling Midtown Atlanta and offering easy access for myriad activities. Dogs are always welcome here, and a large dog park provides ample room for your furry family member to get some exercise. Multi-use paths wind throughout the park, following the rolling topography and dispersing the many visitors to places near and far. Make sure you have a map handy, as the trails change directions often and while you might see the destination you are trying to reach, the actual path to get there can be complicated. The southern end of the park is anchored by a large lake, playground, and the **Piedmont Park Aquatic Center** (piedmontpark.org/aquatics-pool, 404-875-7275), which offers a splash pad and large public pool. There are plenty of shaded spots for a picnic at the edge of the lake, just make sure the ducks and geese don't grab your sandwich. If it's a Saturday

Located right next to downtown Atlanta, Piedmont Park offers abundant greenspace for residents and visitors.

during the warmer months, you might check out the **Green Market** (piedmontpark.org/green-market, 404-875-7275), a large farmers' market that offers food, live music, and activities for the kids.

Heading north through the park takes you past numerous ball fields, tennis courts, and some wetlands, eventually giving way to the **Atlanta Botanical Gardens** (atlantabg.org, 404-876-5859), which occupies a large swath of Piedmont Park. Here you will find trees, bushes, flowers, and other fauna native to Georgia and far beyond. Part adventure, part science, and part art, the gardens are easily accessible from the park itself and provide an immersive experience for the entire family. A children's garden offers numerous hands-on and interactive exhibits for the little ones, and a 600-foot-long canopy walk, soaring 40 feet above the ground, will grab the attention of just about any visitor.

Live music is another staple of Piedmont Park, offering free performances by the Atlanta Symphony Orchestra as well as the annual Midtown Music Festival, which brings hundreds of thousands of attendees to listen to 20 or 30 acts from around the world. The weekly Sunset Sessions music series runs for six months at the **Park Tavern** (park-tavern.com, 404-249-0001), offering alternative music to patrons of the venerable restaurant that has patio seating, welcomes dogs, and provides a nice selection of premium bar food and beverages.

Skyscrapers tower over the athletic fields at Piedmont Park.

One of the greatest stadiums in the entire world has recently opened in downtown Atlanta.

parks, and a wide range of art installations along the route. The trail will eventually encircle the city of Atlanta and link with the existing MARTA rail system, providing easy and environmentally-friendly pedestrian access to vast parts of the metropolis. Streetcar lines are also being established to further expand transportation options for commuters and visitors. As the trails expand, so do the shopping and dining options that are constructed to provide added convenience and accessibility. If the weather is nice, grab a bike or a pair of running shoes and head out for some exercise and maybe a bite to eat. *beltline.org, (404) 477-3003*

MERCEDES-BENZ STADIUM, ATLANTA

One of the most impressive stadiums in the entire world opened its doors in the summer of 2017. The $1.5 billion structure (that's not a typo) contains state-of-the-art everything; no expense was spared, except for the cost of refreshments. The stadium quickly gained a far-reaching reputation as a fan-friendly establishment due to the very reasonable prices charged for food and drink throughout the building. Immediately after it opened, it became a popular destination for hosting worldwide events, including the 2019 Super Bowl. If you have the chance to catch some MLS soccer (Atlanta United) or NFL football (Atlanta Falcons), go for it. Or you can just show up and take a tour of the impressive facility, including a glimpse into the locker rooms and a stroll across the field. Depending on the weather, the extraordinary roof (a true feat of modern engineering) might be open or closed, ensuring comfort year-round. *mercedesbenz stadium.com, (470) 341-5000*

OUTDOORS ATLANTA

Considering the breadth of Atlanta, as well as the overall population of the metropolitan area, you might think you need to make a day trip to get out of the city to enjoy some fresh air. However, one of the biggest advantages of the city is that it is not constrained by any landforms or bodies of water, allowing it to expand naturally into the rest of Georgia. Proper planning means the city hasn't overrun some of the gorgeous natural areas found nearby. Instead these areas have remained little oases surrounded by urban development. Many of the most popular trails and recreation areas are centered around the scenic Chattahoochee River, which gets its start in the mountains and gains considerable volume as it descends to the Gulf of Mexico. As the river passes through the hilly Piedmont of the Atlanta area, the many exposed rocks and boulders contribute to a prevalence of shoals and whitewater that add to the beauty and kayaking opportunities. Listed are a few of the most popular trails and outdoor activities for those living in the Atlanta area. For a full overview of the locations and possibilities to get some fresh air, please visit the excellent Atlanta Trails website (atlantatrails.com), which provides a searchable map to locate trails based on your exact location.

📷 📍 SWEETWATER CREEK STATE PARK

If you head west from downtown Atlanta, you will be greeted with lots of traffic and asphalt that stretches in every direction. But get a little ways outside the perimeter and the sprawl gives way to the natural beauty that thrived throughout the

There are plenty of trails within 30 minutes of downtown Atlanta.

area for millions of years before it was bulldozed and paved. One popular destination is this 2,500-acre park that sits 15 miles from downtown. Boulders, tumbling water, and the fantastic ruins of an old mill set the stage for a wealth of recreational opportunities. A lake gives visitors a chance to enjoy a variety of watersports, while miles of hiking trails wind their way through the thick forest and along the churning water of the creek. Perhaps the centerpiece of the park is the immense ruins of the old New Manchester Mill, which was destroyed in the Civil War. The picturesque remains have served as a backdrop for many a photo, as well as a filming location for the blockbuster movie *The Hunger Games*. *gastate parks.org/sweetwatercreek*, (770) 732-5871

Late day sun streams through the thick forest.

🏞 PALISADES

There are two trails here, each around four miles in length. The trails trace the scenic Chattahoochee River, with one on the east side and one on the west. This general location offers access to Class I and II whitewater, so you are likely to spot a few kayaks or canoes in the water. Each trail is dog-friendly, moderately difficult, and easy to do in a few hours. The East Palisades Trail has some up and down, but it is well worth it for the views of the city in the distance. There are several trail intersections here, but follow the signs carefully and you should be fine. The West Palisades Trail gives a different perspective of the same river. It also has some elevation gain, but the hike isn't bad at all and it includes several beautiful spots

that overlook the shoals and white-water of the river, including a sandy beach where you can easily dip your toes and cool off for a bit.

CASCADE SPRINGS NATURE PRESERVE

Atlanta is big, busy, hectic, and has some serious traffic almost every day of the year. So at times it's natural to want to escape it all, but you don't always have the time to head to the mountains or one of the nearby state parks. When you only have an hour or two to kill, then this is your spot. An unassuming parking lot belies the treasure you will find inside: more than a hundred acres of natural beauty, including a waterfall and Civil War ruins. The hike is hilly but short, and it is just long enough to stretch your legs and enjoy the tranquil surroundings of this small oasis that sits west of downtown. *(404) 546-6744*

📷 SOPE CREEK TRAIL

An easy hike short enough for the whole family, yet beautiful enough to capture your imagination, this trail is located between Marietta and Sandy Springs and is centered around the ruins of a paper mill from the 1800s. Like many structures from that time,

Sope Creek crashes over boulders under colorful trees.

A bamboo forest stretches to the sky on the East Palisades Trail.

it was destroyed by Union troops, but the result is an idyllic setting of boulders, a pond, a burbling stream, and the ruins that are slowly and methodically being reclaimed by nature. Enjoy the shade from the thick canopy of trees and watch the turtles and frogs swim about in the pond's clear waters.

INDIAN SEATS

If you want the feel of the mountains without heading all the way to north Georgia, then this is a great trail on which to get your boots dirty. Located near the city of Cumming, the trail gains some elevation as you head around and up Sawnee Mountain before finally coming to a rocky overlook at the summit. From here you can see the distant Appalachian Mountains, as well as a vast landscape with a color palette that changes by the season. Many a selfie has been taken here, as the rocks create a perfect perch from which to take in the grandeur of Georgia. Plan on spending a bit of time at the top before descending to the parking area.

VICKERY CREEK TRAIL

Hikers and photographers flock to this picturesque trail located close to Roswell. The hike itself shouldn't be a challenge for most, but allow for plenty of time due to the serenity and history of the location. In the 1800s, two mills and a dam were built along the creek to provide supplies to the Confederacy during the Civil War. They were eventually destroyed by Union forces, but the remnants are still visible and provide a striking contrast to the constant flow of Vickery Creek.

SILVER COMET TRAIL

For pedestrians and cyclists, there are few better paths in Georgia than this 61-mile-long paved trail that runs from Atlanta to the Alabama state line. Along the way, you can enjoy a tranquil retreat from motorized traffic, and all of the danger that comes with it. Passing through a mix of urban areas, neighborhoods, and the serene countryside, you have ample opportunities to get some exercise and explore a part of the state that

Vickery Creek is a photographer's paradise just outside of downtown Roswell.

is practically inaccessible by car. If you are feeling particularly ambitious, you can continue on the trail once you reach the Alabama state line, where it turns into the Chief Ladiga Trail for another 33 miles before ending in Anniston. There are several bike shops along the trail if you want to rent some wheels for the day, including **Cycology Bike Shop** (cycologybikeshop.com, 678-909-2472) near Hiram. *silvercometga.com*

📷 🛶 OLD ROPE MILL, WOODSTOCK

An assortment of mountain biking trails await visitors to this picturesque park in Woodstock. Miles of trails challenge beginner and intermediate riders as they wind through the Piedmont woods and along the shores of the Little River that borders the property. While these mountain bike trails are one of the main attractions,

nature lovers will also appreciate the hiking trails and interesting points of interest that can be found throughout the park. An old mill, decommissioned train trestle, and a waterfall that you can paddle to are all a recipe for a relaxing day in the great outdoors. *woodstock.gov/307/olde-rope-mill-park, (770) 517-6788*

ATLANTA NEIGHBORHOODS

The thriving city of Atlanta is not just skyscrapers and unending traffic; it is an assemblage of neighborhoods with very distinct personalities and a lot of pride. Most have locally owned restaurants, bars, and retail stores that provide plenty of character and charm. The lines between each of the many neighborhoods are not always perfectly defined, so it is easy to pass from one neighborhood into the next

The Three Rocks

Georgia has some fascinating geology throughout the state, stretching from the incomprehensively old Appalachian Mountains of the north to the coastal plain of the south, once an ocean and now a flat landscape of fertile soil that produces a large variety of crops. Atlanta sits just to the south of the Appalachian foothills, consisting of hilly terrain and an eclectic assortment of fauna that flourishes in the area. Rising out of the topography are three distinct rock formations, all considered granite monadnocks.

Stone Mountain

Reaching straight into the sky from a relatively flat landscape, this massive dome-shaped geological phenomenon is comprised mostly of quartz. With an elevation of just over 1,000 feet, the rock provides a centerpiece for the surrounding 3,200 acres of beauty. The location offers numerous recreational opportunities along with festivals, light shows, a winter wonderland, two hotels, and a sprawling campground with first-rate amenities.

The mountain itself dates back to long before humans walked this earth. Part of the southern Appalachians, it has towered over the area for millions of years, watching as the surrounding forests slowly succumbed to human development. Speaking of altering the landscape, the stone face was carved multiple times throughout the 1900s, resulting in an homage to three central figures of the Confederacy—Jefferson Davis, Robert E. Lee, and Thomas "Stonewall"

DID YOU KNOW? While Stone Mountain might be one of the largest exposed pieces of granite in the world, what many don't know is that shrimp live on top of the mountain. Nope, not in an aquarium, but in the many depressions that are filled with rain water. The tiny fairy shrimp thrive after heavy rains, leaving eggs behind that ensure future generations will hatch and grow on this rock that sits almost 250 miles from the ocean.

Stretching high above the surrounding hillside, Stone Mountain is a popular destination for Atlanta residents.

Jackson. This carving has come under fire in recent years, with several petitions calling for its removal.

The park itself is a mix of attractions, rides, and natural splendor. If you want some exercise, the hike to the top will certainly get your heart pounding. The path varies between steep and steeper, but once you reach the summit, the views and expansive rock make the endeavor well worthwhile. Fortunately, if you aren't interested in that level of exercise, a Skyride Cable Car runs from the bottom to the top, providing views and air conditioning to visitors onboard. Once at the top, visitors can explore the rock and soak in views of Atlanta to the south and the Appalachian Mountains to the north.

The mountain is only part of the allure of the park, as there are numerous attractions for the entire family. A theme park, scenic railroad, splash pad, 3D movie theater, and plenty of dining options are enough to keep everyone entertained through the day and into the night, when the laser light show illuminates the side of the mountain. Many festivals are held throughout the year, ranging from historical and cultural celebrations to the creation of Snow Mountain, a tubing paradise with acres of manmade snow. The park is open year-round and gets quite busy on the weekends, but the size and breadth of the space helps to alleviate some of the congestion. *stonemountainpark .com, 800-401-2407*

Arabia Mountain National Heritage Area

If Stone Mountain sounds a little too crowded, and a little too developed, Arabia Mountain, about 11 miles to the south, might be more to your liking. You will notice the difference immediately, as it is one of only three National Heritage Areas in Georgia and the primary focus is on conservation. Thirty miles of paths allow visitors broad access to this massive granite rock that rises to 955 feet above sea level. The unyielding surface of the rock gives life to a host of fauna that doesn't exist anywhere else in the state. Perhaps most striking is the brilliant red diamorpha that grows in the numerous small ponds scattered throughout the area. Once a year this explosion of color transforms the mountain, with the red eventually trans-

Distinctive red flowers bloom every spring throughout Arabia Mountain.

forming into white blossoms. No matter when you arrive, the fascinating landscape and extensive views will be well worth the visit. *arabiaalliance.org, (404) 998-8384*

Panola Mountain State Park

While you can't actually hike Panola Mountain without a guide, there are plenty of recreational opportunities here to keep a family occupied. Boating, fishing, archery, a fitness trail, and a playground all provide ways to get some exercise along with fresh air. There is also a small campground for those who want to stick around for a night or two and sleep under the stars. It is primitive and requires a short hike from the parking area, but could be a great segue for those who haven't done a lot of camping. The lake and slow-moving river provide a welcome habitat for a variety of birds, too. *gastateparks.org/panola mountain, (770) 389-7801*

Virginia Highlands offers a trendy mix of shopping, dining, and nightlife.

without even knowing it. There are many neighborhoods throughout the Atlanta area, and a few are highlighted below.

VIRGINIA HIGHLANDS

Enchanting homes, beautiful oak trees, and a flourishing bar scene are hallmarks of this affluent community northeast of downtown Atlanta. A streetcar line in the 1800s helped establish this neighborhood, and what followed was prosperous development, then economic decline, and now a resurgence that has made it one of the most popular neighborhoods in Atlanta. If you are a foodie, you will not leave disappointed. Grab some incredible Italian food from **La Tavola** (latavolatrattoria.com, 404-873-5430) or dine on the sidewalk at **Murphy's** (murphysatlanta

.com, 404-872-0904). If you would like to grab a drink in a relaxed environment, the dive-bar atmosphere of **Moe's & Joe's** (404-873-6090) should fit the bill nicely. Want some blues to feed your soul? Check out **Blind Willie's** (blindwilliesblues.com, 404-873-2583), which features live blues music every night. Live-music fanatics might have heard of **Smith's Olde Bar** (smithsoldebar.com, 404-875-1522), which has seen the likes of John Mayer and Widespread Panic on its stage. Located just north of Virginia Highlands, this hot spot almost always offers music to enjoy throughout the week. A spacious bar and tons of pool tables also add to the evening's possibilities. *virginiahigh land.com*

OLD FOURTH WARD

Modern culture collides with a fascinating history in this beautiful neighborhood that has seen a resurgence since the 1960s. Perhaps most famous as the neighborhood where Martin Luther King Jr. grew up, the area is now an alluring collection of renovated warehouses, high-end retail shops, beautiful lofts, and mouthwatering restaurants. Getting here is pretty easy, as you can take a car, the Atlanta BeltLine, or the Atlanta Streetcar. Once you are in the area, take a stroll and explore the neighborhood's iconic locations such as the **Jackson Street Bridge,** which provides a picturesque view of the downtown skyline. There are plenty of great restaurants in this neighborhood, but one of the most popular is the original **Thumbs Up Diner** (thumbsupdiner.com, 404-223-0690), which is famous for its breakfasts. Open until mid-afternoon every day, this place serves up food not easily forgotten (the same goes for the wait

Jackson Street Bridge offers visitors to the Old Fourth Ward an excellent view of the downtown skyline.

on the weekend). Make sure you bring your cash though, as they don't take credit cards or checks. For nightlife, the Old Fourth Ward doesn't disappoint. If you aren't sure what you want to get into, just head down to Edgewood Avenue, where bars and clubs line several city blocks. For a really cool vibe and an homage to the popular television show *Twin Peaks*, stop by **The Book House Pub** (the bookhousepub.net, 404-254-1176) and grab one of their creative mixed drinks (the vodka-heavy Backstreet Morning is a good start to your night) as you soak up the atmosphere. If grooving to a DJ in an intimate atmosphere is more your thing, the electric ambiance at **The Sound Table** (the soundtable.com, 404-835-2534) is guaranteed to get your heart pumping. If you love video games mixed with a bit of nostalgia, then the **Joystick Gamebar** (joystickgamebar.com, 404-525-3002) is a fantastic place to grab a beer and challenge your friends to a game of Galaga.

GRANT PARK

Historic homes surround a sprawling, beautiful greenspace in this popular park that sits just southeast of the downtown area. Most visitors come for **Zoo Atlanta** (zooatlanta.org, 404-624-9453), but there is certainly more to experience while you are in the area. The 131-acre park is the epicenter of the neighborhood, with vast numbers of hardwood trees that provide plenty of needed shade in the summer. This area is one of the oldest in the city, and you'll discover craftsman-style homes that were constructed in the late 1800s and early 1900s. If you don't want to visit the zoo, you can still enjoy the great outdoors through the extensive sidewalk system that winds its way through the park and the historic neighborhoods. There are plenty of options for

Downtown Atlanta rises above the trees of Grant Park.

dining and drinks, including a rooftop with a view at the **Six Feet Under Pub & Fish House** (sixfeetunder.net, 404-810-0040) or a fantastic glass of wine in the cozy **Ziba's Restaurant and Wine Bar** (404-622-4440). If you are on the north end of the park, grab a bite at **Dakota Blue** (dakotablueatlanta.com, 404-589-8002), a Mexican and Cuban restaurant with outside seating. *grantpark.org*

CASTLEBERRY HILL

Huge warehouses and industrial areas once dominated this neighborhood that sits mere blocks from the State Capitol and the massive Mercedes-Benz Stadium. With so many popular attractions just a short walk away, it's no wonder that this area has

been the focus of massive revitalization efforts over the past decade. A mix of art galleries, restaurants, gorgeous loft apartments, and massive Hollywood productions have all

Castleberry Hill is fast becoming an art destination in Atlanta.

contributed to its reputation as one of the up-and-coming neighborhoods in the city. The entire area is very walkable, and a relaxing wander takes you past colorful buildings, murals, and stunning art galleries that beg you to step inside. In fact, if you are around on the second Friday of the month, you should join the art stroll, which features an art-themed block party. If you are a movie buff, consider a walking tour with **Atlanta Movie Tours** (atlantamovietours.com, 855-255-3456), which gives you access to the filming locations for a wide variety of Hollywood blockbusters, including *Stranger Things, The Hunger Games, Black Panther,* and *The Walking Dead.* Of course, a neighborhood can't thrive if there aren't any good places to eat, and fortunately that isn't an issue here. Considering America's love of Mexican food, it's no wonder the **No Mas Cantina** (nomascantina.com, 404-574-5678) is such a huge hit. Vibrant colors, thoughtful design, and mouth-watering tacos ensure the locals keep coming back to this massive restaurant, complete with a large artisan market and a separate café offering coffee and breakfast. If you're there late, the bar will not disappoint, spanning almost the length of the restaurant and then spilling out to a large outdoor patio with a perfect atmosphere. Not too many restaurants can claim to be an integral part of American history, but **Paschal's** (paschalsatlanta.com, 404-525-2023) can. The restaurant served as a meeting location for Dr. Martin Luther King Jr. and other civil rights leaders due to its anti-segregation policies, eventually becoming the unofficial headquarters for the Civil Rights Movement. The restaurant has since moved locations, but the recipes remain the same. Today, patrons

are greeted by striking historic photographs and highly satisfying soul food, including some memorable fried chicken. *castleberryhill.org*

DECATUR

Plenty of beauty along with a bustling intellectual community compose the fabric of this neighborhood that sits to the east of downtown Atlanta. Home to both Emory University and Agnes Scott College, the neighborhood caters to a diverse population of college students, professors, and working professionals. The result is an eclectic mix of bars, restaurants, retail, and greenspace. Throw in some of the best schools in the city, and it's no wonder that more than 18,000 residents have flocked to this four-square mile mecca. If it's a nice day, take a stroll through the campus of **Emory University** (emory.edu, 404-727-6123), one of the most respected institutions of higher education in the country. The 630-acre campus is wooded and features a wide range of striking buildings that are frequented by the 14,000 students who attend school there. If you enjoy live music, then an essential visit should be **Eddie's Attic** (eddiesattic.com, 404-377-4976), which has been the launching point for countless musical acts. If you have ever listened to John Mayer, the Black Crowes, or Justin Bieber, you have an idea of the performances that have graced the intimate stage of this music club in downtown Decatur. For a truly Decatur dining experience, grab a drink and a meal at **Leon's Full Service** (leonsfullservice, 404-687-0500), a meticulously converted gas station that now features a striking outdoor patio and spacious bar. A hot spot for the locals, the establishment features an extensive food and drink menu as well as a

Decatur enjoys plenty of culture and a youthful vibe, courtesy of nearby Emory University.

bocce ball pit that provides plenty of entertainment for the patrons. **The Iberian Pig** (theiberianpigatl.com, 404-371-8800) offers a memorable dining experience full of savory tapas and hard-to-replicate ambiance. Ever had a bacon-wrapped Medjool date? That might change after your visit. *decaturga.com, 404-370-4100*

DEKALB FARMERS MARKET

This venerable market has housed the wares from locations near and far for over 40 years, providing one of the most diverse collections of food, wine, coffee, and flowers in the southeast. Every day fresh fish is delivered from around the globe, along with cheese, vegetables, fruit, and a host of other goods you might never have heard of. Even if you aren't preparing a single meal during your travels, the experience of visiting this market is worth a trip. You're almost guaranteed to hear several different languages as you walk the aisles and decide which of the mouth-watering chocolates you want to try. If nothing else, head over to the bakery and pick up a few fresh pastries that were baked that morning. For those who don't have a kitchen handy, step into the restaurant for a meal that features ingredients straight from the shelves of this world market. *dekalb farmersmarket.com, (404) 377-6400*

OUTSIDE THE PERIMETER

Making recommendations for places to visit outside the perimeter (outside Interstate 285) is always a challenge. There are so many cities and so many offerings that it takes a lot to stand out. Here are some unique destinations worth the drive that also give you an excuse to explore the surrounding area. You'll find a nice

Buford Highway (Foodie Highway)

Leaving Buckhead and heading northeast into the suburbs, Buford Highway (colloquially known as "BuHi") is as essential a road to foodies as it is to Atlanta commuters. With more than a hundred restaurants concentrated along a length of seven miles, the road serves as the epicenter of an immigration movement. Entrepreneurs hailing from the far reaches of the globe have opened shops and restaurants along this piece of asphalt, creating an impromptu cultural highway where one can dine on Sichuan delicacies from China, Bagladeshi cuisine, and seafood specialties from Mexico's Pacific Coast. You could spend months exploring the restaurants along this road and never eat the same thing twice, but here are a few notables to get you started.

Food Terminal

Malaysian cuisine abounds at this hip, modern establishment that showcases Asian street foods. You know you are somewhere special when you sit down at the table and they hand you a menu that looks like a book. The highly diverse entrees are infused with unique flavors many diners have never experienced, contributing to the restaurant's critical acclaim and popularity. Make sure you leave room for dessert, as treats like the Mango Grapefruit will ensure you remember this dining experience for a long time. *food-terminal.com, (678) 353-6110*

Havana Sandwich Shop

Want an authentic Cuban Sandwich that ticks all of the required boxes to satisfy your palette? Look no farther than this establishment that has been serving up some of Cuba's best food since the mid 1970s. Order a side of *Maduros* (sweet plantains) to go with the Cuban, then wash it all down with a fresh *Batido* (milkshake) to complete a meal that's easy on the wallet and hard on the urge to order even more. *havanaatlanta .com, (404) 636-4094*

A hip and modern interior complements the dining experience at Food Terminal.

Authentic Mexican food at El Rey del Taco brings people from near and far.

El Rey del Taco
Made-from-scratch corn tortillas (ask for them—they are worth the extra cost) filled with a variety of meat, onions, and cilantro ensure that these will be some of the best, and most authentic, Mexican tacos you ever put in your mouth. If you're feeling adventurous, go for the goat or beef cheek, both of which have plentiful seasoning and provide a taco experience you won't find at your normal Mexican joint. If you'd rather go the seafood route, you'll find plenty of choices on the menu. *elreydeltacoatl.com, (770) 986-0032*

Gu's Kitchen
The Sichuan region of China provides some delectable cuisine, and it is recreated faithfully at this counter-service restaurant near Doraville. Noodles and dumplings are the specialty, and as you might expect, they are worth the wait. If you like spicy food, this is a required stop on your BuHi journey, as much of the menu ranges from hot to extreme. *guskitchen.com, (470) 299-2388*

Starr's Mill is one part history, and many parts beauty.

combination of dining, shopping, recreation, and history. These towns and cities used to be surrounded by undeveloped countryside and the historic squares, interesting architecture, and downtown walkability make for an interesting outing (perhaps even an overnight).

📷 STARR'S MILL, FAYETTEVILLE

Considering the importance of cotton, lumber, and textiles in the 1800s, it's no wonder there are so many mills scattered across Georgia. Many have fallen into disrepair, which makes this one all the more special. The picturesque structure sits right on the banks of Whitewater Creek, where it was originally constructed as a grist mill. Fires claimed the first two mills, but the current one was built in 1907 and still stands today. This little slice of history is worth a visit for the photographs, as well as the relaxing

sounds emanating from the waterfall.

LANIER ISLANDS, BUFORD

When Atlanta residents want to escape to the lake, many of them head to nearby Lake Lanier, an expansive manmade reservoir to the northeast of Atlanta. While there are plenty of boat ramps, fishing piers, and multimillion-dollar homes dotting its shores, perhaps the most popular destination is the family-friendly resort that features golf, dining, accommodations, and the sprawling Jimmy Buffet–inspired Margaritaville. Guests can cool off in the water park, zip-line over the lake, or relax on the vast manmade beach while watching high-dollar yachts float by. If you get hungry you can satisfy your hunger (and quench your thirst) at the **Landshark Bar and Grill** (470-323-3440), which sits right on the beach. *lanier islands.com, (770) 945-8787*

📷 KENNESAW MOUNTAIN NATIONAL BATTLEFIELD PARK, KENNESAW

What is now a peaceful and scenic expanse of woods and fields was once the site of a bloody confrontation between 160,000 Union and Confederate soldiers. There is plenty of history to go along with the natural beauty you'll find when you visit this location north of Atlanta. Almost 3,000 acres offer miles of hiking and biking, and you'll find quite a view at the top of Kennesaw Mountain. But perhaps the most important component of this experience is the recognition of one of the darkest times in the nation's history and the loss of 5,350 soldiers who perished here. The visitor's center offers a 35-minute movie about the battle along with a museum full of artifacts. *nps.gov/ kemo, (770) 427-4686*

A civil war cannon sits outside of the entrance to the museum at Kennesaw Mountain.

It's hard to ignore the impact of the headstones when you visit Marietta National Cemetery.

MARIETTA NATIONAL CEMETERY, MARIETTA

A peaceful and somber remembrance of the thousands of soldiers who gave their lives during the Civil War, this cemetery is a beautiful location to take a walk and gain a better understanding of the true cost of the war. With close to 20,000 internments (many from the nearby Battle of Kennesaw Mountain), this cemetery is wonderfully preserved and manicured. You will be struck by the sheer number of headstones along with how quiet the area is. Located in the middle of the city, the cemetery is a draw for visitors and history-buffs throughout the United States. *cem .va.gov/cems/nchp/marietta.asp, 866-236-8159*

CHATTAHOOCHEE NATURE CENTER, ROSWELL

The combination of this family-friendly destination along with the many offerings of nearby Roswell is a recipe for a fun family outing. Nestled on the banks of the Chattahoochee River, the nature center offers a variety of educational opportunities for people of all ages, along with activities such as canoeing, zip-lining, and nature walks. The picturesque location and commitment to conservation brings visitors from all over the Atlanta area, and countless shopping and dining opportunities in Roswell keep them coming back. *chattnature center.org, 770-992-2055*

BAPS SHRI SWAMINARAYAN MANDIR, LILBURN

If exploring breathtaking cultural destinations is something that interests

Château Elan

Everyone deserves a bit of pampering now and then, and this sprawling property outside of Atlanta offers many ways to relax and unwind. A day of sampling succulent wine and fresh cuisine on this French-style estate is an enticing prospect for those who want to get away from the stress of daily life. There are a variety of accommodations for even the most discerning guests, with attractions that include horseback riding, wine tastings, championship golf, and a 35,000-square-foot European-style spa that provides meals, lodging, and complete body rejuvenation.

If you want to go back to the roots of this world-class establishment, you can quite literally trace them back to the grapes growing in the vineyard. Initially planted in the 1980s, the grapes have paved the way for a destination winery that has seen expansive growth across its rolling 3,500 acres south of the Appalachians. Wine tastings (Tuesday through Sunday) provide a sample of the large variety of wines fermented on site using grapes grown in the fields, as well as those flown in from other locations. A small-plate menu is available to mollify your appetite, or you can head to one of the numerous restaurants for a greater variety of mouth-watering dishes. It doesn't matter if you are craving a fresh Guinness with classic fish and chips or meticulously prepared fresh seafood, the dining options are plentiful. From fine dining to a poolside bar, no matter where you are at the resort a good meal is waiting nearby.

If you love golf, then 36 holes of championship golf provide plenty of challenges for golfers of all abilities. If you prefer to work on your short game, then the par-three course will more than suffice. The undulating terrain, manicured greens, and intriguing layouts of both the Chateau and Woodlands courses ensure a fun outing for golfers of all abilities.

After a day of golfing, horseback riding, lounging by the pool, tasting wine, and getting a massage, you will likely be exhausted and need a place to lay your head. Depending on your priorities, a luxurious inn, golf villas, and rooms at the spa are available. This is a destination in every sense of the word—come for an afternoon or a week without ever needing to leave. *chateauelan.com, (678) 425-0900*

For pampering, wine, and lots of golf, it's hard to beat Chateau Elan.

Another day begins in Atlanta.

you, this location is worth every minute in the car from downtown Atlanta. The largest Hindu temple in the United States is impressive in size and scale, but perhaps most astonishing is how it was assembled. Over 34,000 pieces of Italian marble, Turkish limestone, and Indian pink sandstone were all carved by hand in India before being shipped to Atlanta for assembly. You can spend hours touring the inside and outside of this architectural masterpiece, which is free to the public. A modest dress code is required and the shrines are only open certain times each day, so check the website before you head over. *baps.org, (678) 906-2277*

SIX FLAGS OVER GEORGIA, AUSTELL

Not far from Atlanta sits a massive theme park that can provide plenty of excitement for the entire family. For over half a century, Six Flags has given adrenaline junkies a destination full of rollercoasters and other thrill rides that get the heart pounding and fill the air with screams of excitement. In addition to the 11 gravity-defying roller-ercoasters, there are family-friendly rides and even a waterpark with slides and a wave pool. Park hours change with the season, so check the website before you go. *sixflags.com/overgeorgia, (770) 739-3400*

Cows graze next to an abandoned house.

CENTRAL GEORGIA

Certainly the most densely populated area of Georgia is concentrated in the northern half of the state. The Atlanta metro area encompasses well over 8,000 square miles and continues to expand, swallowing once sleepy towns and injecting business and industry

Fields of green are a staple of Central Georgia.

Brilliant leaves can be found all over the state in the fall.

into the local economies. As you move south and cross below Interstate 20, you'll detect an almost palpable change in the landscape, the level of activity, the amount of development, and the general way of life. Gone is the gridlock and twice daily traffic jams that plague one of the fastest growing cities in the United States. With the exception of larger cities like Augusta, Macon, and Columbus, you'll find very little traffic and more expansive swaths of land, many of which have been handed down through generations of families.

The roads are a little straighter, the topography a little flatter, and the creeks and rivers a little muddier, but there is still plenty of beauty and numerous destinations for your enjoyment. It might be tempting to jump on Interstate 75 and bypass much of this part of the state, but you will be missing out on an area rich with history. Antebellum homes abound, even in the tiniest towns. Agriculture is omnipresent, the lifeblood of the state of Georgia since its inception. Sherman and his massive army marched right through the heart of this area 150 years ago, burning and decimating almost everything in sight as he pillaged his way to Savannah. You'll encounter plenty of historical markers and locations that tell the story, along with many buildings that withstood the onslaught.

Georgia's designated Lake Country is here, with two massive lakes that provide ample recreation opportunities both on and off the water. Though it can get hot in the middle of summer, for the majority of the year you'll appreciate the temperate climate where you can get outside and enjoy the sunshine, even in the dead of winter. Outdoorsmen travel here from hours or even days away for the abundant hunting and fishing; in fact, at times, there appear to be more deer than people.

So, get out of the city, slow things down, explore the towns interspersed across the forested landscape, and soak in some of the Southern charm that positively oozes from the friendly and welcoming people who live here. It is a great place to explore if you are traveling between the mountains and the coast, and country roads are far more interesting than the interminable asphalt of the major interstates.

An old barn sits alone in a field of brilliant green.

Libations in Central Georgia

Augusta
Savannah River Brewing Co.
savannahriverbrew.com

Carrollton
Printer's Ale Mfg.
printers-ale.com

Columbus
Cannon Brew Pub
thecannonbrewpub.com

Guyton
Butterducks Winery
butterduckswinery.com

Hampton
Jailhouse Brewing
jailhousebrewing.com

LaGrange
Beacon Brewing Co.
beacon.beer

Wild Leap Brew Company
wildleap.com

Macon
Piedmont Brewery & Kitchen
piedmontbrewery.com

Newnan
Abide Brewing Co.
abidebrewingco.com

Omaha
Omaha Brewing Co.
omahabrewingcompany.com

Peachtree City
Line Creek Brewing Co.
linecreekbrewing.com

Statesboro
Eagle Creek
eaglecreekbrewingco.com

Meinhardt Vineyards and Winery
meinhardtvineyards.com

Sparta
Cedar Green Vineyards
cedargreenvineyards.com

Courson's Winery
(706) 444-0616

Warm Springs
Warm Springs Vineyard and Winery
(706) 655-2233

West Point
Chattabrewchee Southern Brewhouse
chattabrewchee.com

River's Bend Winery and Vineyard
riversbendwineryga.com

White Plains
Springtale Winery and Vineyards
springtale.com

🐺 HISTORIC BANNING MILLS, WHITESBURG

For adrenaline junkies, there are few destinations in the state that will get the heart pounding more than this self-described "Adventure Resort" in western Georgia. Located at the site of an old mill town on the scenic Snake Creek, this place has plenty of activities to keep you occupied for hours or even days. The centerpiece is their massive zip line course (literally the largest in the world) that has you racing above and through the trees at speeds up to 70 miles per hour. With almost 7 miles—yes, miles—of zip lines snaking through the forest, it would take you 12 hours to complete them all. The resort also houses the world's tallest artificial climbing wall, which towers over 135 feet and challenges even the most experienced climbers. If you want to really have time to explore all of the amenities, there are options for overnight lodging, including tree houses nestled in the shade. *historicbanningmills .com, (770) 834-9149*

GREAT WOLF LODGE, LAGRANGE

Are there adventure-loving members of your family? Do you love hurtling down water slides at high speed with friends and family? Is it January? Don't worry, this 93,000-thousand-square-foot indoor water park has you covered, literally. The massive heated space provides plenty of fun for the family, no matter what the age. The water is 84°F year-round, ensuring comfort along with the heart-pumping adventure. There's a lot more than just water slides though, you'll find a playground/splash pad, a wave pool, a large outdoor pool, and even a pool (with several slides) for the youngest members of your family. Restaurants, shopping, and non-swimsuit attractions, such as an arcade and mini-golf course,

No matter what time of the year, you can frolic in the water at Great Wolf Lodge.

It's easy to see why President FDR loved to have lunch at this location.

Thousands of butterflies fill the air at the Cecil B. Day Butterfly Center.

provide more entertainment even after you dry off. A massive hotel completes the experience, giving you the convenience of a comfortable bed to rest your body after a full day of excitement. *greatwolf.com, (844) 473-9653*

📷 🌳 F.D. ROOSEVELT STATE PARK, PINE MOUNTAIN

This state park, located just outside FDR's vacation home in Warm Springs, offers a wide range of activities for those who love fresh air and the serenity of nature. Over 40 miles of trails wind through the park, with the longest being the 23-mile Pine Mountain Trail. Though the terrain in central Georgia is more piedmont than mountain, there is a fair amount of elevation in this area. The park is over 9,000 acres in size and features a wide variety of activities, including camping, horseback riding, kayaks, canoes, and a swimming pool. Not to be missed is Dowdell's Knob, a beautiful overlook where FDR frequently had picnics. *gastateparks.org/fdroosevelt, (706) 663-4858*

🌳 CALLAWAY GARDENS, PINE MOUNTAIN

This sprawling resort located near the Alabama state line is brimming with activities for people of all ages and interests. Located close to FDR State Park, the 2,500-acre location has several hotels, two championship golf courses, miles of trails for walking or bicycling, and fantastic restaurants. Not to be missed is the 7,300-square-foot **Cecil B. Day Butterfly Center,** one of the largest and most impressive butterfly conservatories in North America. Here you can walk among more than a thousand butterflies as they flutter their way throughout the glass building. *callawaygardens.com, 844-512-3826*

THE LITTLE WHITE HOUSE, WARM SPRINGS

President Franklin Delano Roosevelt, like many others during the early 1900s, suffered from the debilitating effects of polio. This incurable disease confined the president to a wheelchair and caused him a great deal of discomfort. In search of a place that could help provide him with relief from the excruciating pain, he discovered Warm Springs and soon found that the warmth from the natural mineral water offered improvement. It helped him so much that he built a small cottage he would visit repeatedly for the rest of his life. Later known as The Little White House, this perfectly preserved home is now filled with historical artifacts and interesting stories about the life and times of President FDR. This state historical site not only hosts the Little White House, but also a guesthouse, slave quarters, and museum dedicated to the accomplishments of our 32nd president. The museum includes several of his favorite cars,

One of the president's favorite cars sits on display inside of the museum.

The Little White House was far from ostentatious, and President FDR spent a lot of time here.

The reflection of color makes the lakes around Georgia perfect for catching a sunset.

Georgia's Seven Natural Wonders

The natural beauty and changing landscape of Georgia are some of its greatest assets, but sometimes it's hard to decide just where to visit. If you enjoy science and geology and like to marvel at nature, then these seven places should be on your list. Each one is covered in the book to provide detail and context about what makes them unique.

- Amicalola Falls
- Okefenokee Swamp
- Stone Mountain
- Providence Canyon
- Radium Springs
- Tallulah Gorge
- Warm Springs

Providence Canyon is one of Seven Natural Wonders in the state of Georgia.

a horse-drawn carriage, and a very thorough biography. *gastateparks.org /littlewhitehouse*, *(706) 655-5870*

WARM SPRINGS

This sleepy farming community became a vacation destination in the 1800s as word spread about the mineral springs that flowed at a constant 88°F from the earth. With better infrastructure and a railroad running from Atlanta, a mere 60 miles away, the town of Warm Springs saw an increase in visitors who were seeking a spa vacation or relief from yellow fever outbreaks along Georgia's coast. By the early 1900s, the increasingly common automobile led to a decline in visitors to the area; the public had newfound freedom to explore and no

longer relied on trains or horses for travel.

Tourism was revitalized in the 1920s after President Franklin D. Roosevelt discovered the town and built the Little White House. Over the coming years, Warm Springs was put back on the map as a therapeutic destination for the many thousands suffering from the debilitating effects of polio. FDR purchased a therapeutic center to help with the treatment of these conditions, and it still exists today as the **Roosevelt Warm Springs Institute for Rehabilitation.** FDR also founded The National Foundation to raise money for Warm Springs and polio victims. This foundation would later become the present-day March of Dimes. Although polio is no longer a major health threat, the foundation now raises money for other diseases such as cancer. Warm Springs is also known as one of Georgia's Seven Wonders because of the 88°F water that bubbles to the surface from 3,800 feet below the ground.

Today, Warm Springs is a classic Southern town with several dining options and locally-owned shops that offer a little bit of everything. While you cannot bathe or swim in the nearby springs, you can feel the warm waters flow over your hand at the **Historic Pools Museum** (706-655-5870), which is included with your visit to the Little White House. While there, you can look over the facilities that offered relief to thousands of visitors, including President Roosevelt, back in the early 1900s. *warm springsga.com, (706) 655-3322*

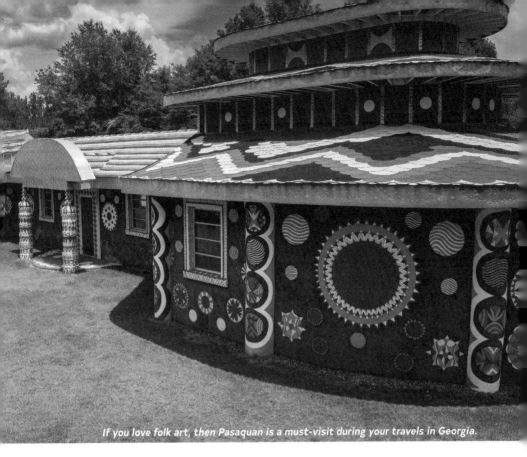

If you love folk art, then Pasaquan is a must-visit during your travels in Georgia.

📷 PASAQUAN, BUENA VISTA

If you like out-of-this-world art, then add this to your list of places to visit when you are in the Columbus area. Eddie Martin was an eccentric man, to put it lightly. This eccentricity led to brilliant, colorful folk art, which is spread over a seven-acre rural piece of land near Buena Vista. There are six main structures along with many other elaborately painted walls and edifices that are a result of a sickness and resulting vision Martin had when living in New York City. This vision brought him back to Georgia and "do something," which began the thirty-year undertaking that transformed the peaceful countryside into a folk-art mecca. Now managed by Columbus State University, the location hosts a variety of events throughout

the year. *pasaquan.columbusstate .edu, (706) 507-8306*

COLUMBUS

There is much to explore in Georgia, but for adventure-lovers, the biggest surprise might come here in Columbus. For years Columbus was thought of as a military town, with the sprawling Fort Benning located just to the southeast of the city. However, smart planning and redevelopment has turned this city on the Alabama border into a destination replete with art, adventure, and abundant history.

When you roll into the downtown area you will notice that it is relatively quiet compared to many cities. Large streets with a mix of new and historic buildings create a grid in the historic area, with many beautiful antebellum

The rising sun fills the sky with shades of pink over downtown Columbus.

homes located a stone's throw from the large buildings that make up downtown. Parking is free and easy to find, and the city is very walkable, with the most active areas within a short stroll from the beautiful river that rolls and tumbles its way through the downtown area. The Columbus Riverwalk provides easy access to the water, and if you really want a close

A Blue Heron fishes the swirling waters of the Chattahoochee in Columbus.

view of the rapids, you can cross over to Waveshaper Island using the footbridge.

With a population of just under 200,000 people, Columbus is not a huge city compared to the enormous metropolis of Atlanta. Its location on the banks of the Chattahoochee River made it a haven for textile companies, and large factories were built along the waterfront. But shipping and production methods have changed with modern technology and the buildings eventually emptied, falling into disrepair. In the 1980s, the local government had the foresight to begin a multi-decade revitalization effort with the aim of transforming the natural resource of the Chatta-hoochee into a desirable attraction. And they succeeded. The Colum-bus Riverwalk, a park, new condos and lofts, and, in 2012 the crowning achievement opened: the longest urban whitewater rafting location in the world. Nowhere else can you find world-class whitewater flowing right through a vibrant downtown. What makes it so unique, and desirable, is the accessibility and adaptability of the whitewater to all skill levels, from novice to expert. A dam-controlled release of water changes throughout the day, with a slow release in the morning (perfect for a safe, family-friendly adventure) to a much higher flow rate in the afternoon, generating Class III to Class V rapids that are some of the biggest in the eastern United States. *visitcolumbusga.com,* *(800) 999-1613*

CHATTAHOOCHEE

WHITEWATER EXPRESS

If it's a warm day and you have a bit of adventure in you, then experiencing the whitewater of the Chattahoochee is a great way to spend a few hours. A guided trip is your best

You can cross the river in a very unique way if you aren't afraid of heights.

bet, and this conveniently located shop offers multiple trips each day. In addition, you can rent a kayak, a stand-up paddleboard (SUP), or a bike, or ride a zip line across the river

Onlookers watch as a raft of adventurers challenges the unforgiving whitewater.

Museums in Columbus

If it's too hot or some rain is falling, there are plenty of indoor things to occupy your time in Columbus.

You will be hard-pressed to find a more engaging and memorable tribute to the US military than the **National Infantry Museum and Soldier Center** (nationalinfantrymuseum.org, 706-685-5800). The 190,000-square-foot facility is filled with immense, interactive exhibits that convey the honor and sacrifice made by the soldiers of this great country. Artifacts, artwork, and military equipment can be found inside and out, and visitors can easily spend a full day here. The IMAX theatre offers military documentaries (as well as select Hollywood films) in 3D, an experience every member of the family can enjoy.

The National Infantry Museum houses an extensive collection of memorabilia.

The **National Civil War Naval Museum** (portcolumbus.org, 706-327-9798) is another place to learn about military history. This museum explores the lesser-known, but quite important, use of ships by both the Union and Confederacy. The Civil War was a turning point in naval warfare with the introduction of ironclad ships and submarines, and visitors can even explore the impressive and substantial remains of the ironclad CSS *Jackson*, on full display in the museum.

If you have some science-lovers in your group, the **Coca-Cola Space Science Center** (ccssc.org, 706-649-1477) will provide them with plenty to do for an afternoon. Interactive exhibits and an extensive collection of NASA artifacts make this a highly educational museum, and it is conveniently located right in the middle of downtown.

from Georgia to Alabama and then back again. *whitewaterexpress.com, (800) 676-7238*

DRAGONFLY TRAILS, COLUMBUS

An extensive network of trails provides access for walking, running, or biking without the danger of motorists. Visitors who want to pedal Columbus and get a bit of exercise have some options. Take in views along the 22-mile Columbus Riverwalk before cutting over to the Fall Line Trace, a rail-to-trail greenway that runs 11 miles between Midland and Columbus. It passes through the picturesque Flat Rock Park as well, providing even more riding possibilities for cyclists. It is a serious draw for the city; visitors arrive daily with bikes in tow to explore the pathways and enjoy the beauty.

THE ROCK RANCH, THE ROCK

S. Truett Cathy not only started Chick-fil-A, he also founded this highly engaging agritourism destination that includes a wide range of activities. The 1,500-acre cattle ranch has a lot more than bovines, including a variety of farm animals, zip lines, pony rides, a miniature train,

The Dragonfly Trails provide a safe and motorist-free path for exploring the Columbus area.

paddle boats, and the popular pedal carts. Many attractions are seasonal, so no matter what time of year you visit, there will be something new and interesting to do. If you want something truly unique, book a night in one of their Conestoga Wagons, a modern replica of the wagons you have seen in virtually every Western movie. Each

Senoia's charming downtown is the filming location for several shows and movies.

wagon has bunkbeds for eight people, providing shelter for the whole family as you sleep out under the stars. *therockranch.com, (706) 647-6374*

SENOIA

This quintessential small, Southern town was put on the world map due to its role in several Hollywood offerings, including *Fried Green Tomatoes, Driving Miss Daisy, Footloose,* and perhaps most notably, *The Walking Dead.* The popular AMC series really transformed the town, utilizing the downtown area along with the surrounding countryside as a backdrop for many of the episodes. A constant influx of tourists and Hollywood stars has brought about a resurgence in the community, with numerous restaurants and shops now catering to these visitors. The town itself is understandably picturesque, hence its popularity among the many directors who have filmed scenes in

Dining in Columbus

After a day of adventure, exercise, and a bit of history, you might have worked up an appetite (and perhaps a bit of thirst). Don't worry, there are plenty of options to satisfy any craving.

Before dinner you can grab a fresh pint at **The Cannon Brew Pub** (thecannonbrew pub.com, 706-653-2337), a microbrewery in the heart of downtown. The Red Jacket Ale is one of their most popular, and an extensive burger menu might keep you there for a meal as well.

If you want to go a little more upscale, it is a short walk to either **The Loft** (theloft .com, 706-596-8141) or **11th and Bay Southern Table** (11thandbay.com, 706-940-0202) for some excellent food. The former has a little something for everyone and the latter offers outdoor seating with easy access to the Riverwalk and Chattahoochee River.

If you'd rather go a little laid back and don't mind getting your fingers dirty, then pick apart some ribs at the **Zombie Pig BBQ** (zombiepigbbq.com, 706-662-0941). When the team isn't competing in BBQ competitions and winning a whole host of awards, they are fixing some of the best pulled pork and ribs you'll find in Georgia.

On the opposite end of the spectrum, you can splurge and have an **Epic** (epiccuisine .com, 706-507-9909) meal at arguably the nicest restaurant in Columbus, located just off of the Chattahoochee River in the heart of downtown. Reservations are recommended; this fine dining experience is a popular one for residents and visitors alike.

the area. More than 25 productions have utilized Senoia thus far, and that number will surely grow. If you are a fan of The Walking Dead then a walking tour through the streets of Senoia makes sense. While several are available, you can't go wrong with the **Big Zombie Walking Tour** (atlantamovie tours.com/tours/big-zombie-tour, 855-255-3456), which lasts an hour and takes you to several recognizable landmarks. If you work up an appetite, you can continue to pay homage to this venerable series by grabbing a drink and some food at **Nic & Norman's** (nicandnormans.com, 770-727-9432), which is owned by the show's special-effects creator Greg Nicotero and star Norman Reedus. Afterward, take a stroll around the charming town, stick your head in a few shops, and keep an eye out for any wayward zombies who have escaped the set. enjoysenoia.net, (770) 727-9173

DAUSET TRAILS NATURE CENTER, JACKSON

There is no cost to visit and enjoy the great outdoors at this non-profit nature center near Jackson. There are a variety of rescued animals that visitors can see and learn about, with almost all of them hailing from the Georgia area. With lots of hiking and biking, a barnyard exhibit, and a nineteenth-century working farm, this is a great spot to relax, refresh, and appreciate the abundance of natural beauty in Georgia. dausettrails .com, (770) 775-6798

HIGH FALLS STATE PARK, JACKSON

Explore more than 1,000 acres at this state park featuring the tallest waterfall south of the Atlanta area. A large river, cascading water, and a lake filled with bass all contribute to

The Whistle Stop Cafe is the centerpiece of the charming town of Juliette.

an outdoor-lover's dream. A campground features waterside yurts that can be rented nightly. History lovers will appreciate the remnants of a hydroelectric plant that operated in the 1800s, and there are almost five miles of trails for those who want to explore the hilly terrain and views across the flowing river. *gastateparks.org*, (478) 993-3053

WHISTLE STOP CAFE, JULIETTE

It's remarkable how much influence Hollywood can have on a local economy, and no town knows it more than Juliette. All but forgotten after the decline of the railroad industry, it was fortunate to be chosen as the filming location for the 1991 hit *Fried Green Tomatoes*. What followed was a full-fledged transformation into a tourist destination, full of shops and art. The centerpiece is this café, which still looks just like the movie set. Have a seat at the counter, order some Southern fare (and, of course, a side of fried green tomatoes), and you might just feel like you have stepped onto the set of a Hollywood classic. *thewhistlestopcafe.com*, (478) 992-8886

JARRELL PLANTATION, JULIETTE

Georgia has a lot of plantations, but not too many are so well-preserved while also allowing public access. This 1,000-acre plantation was owned by the Jarrell family for over 140 years, and multiple buildings were constructed over that time, including a sawmill, cotton gin, gristmill, and sugar cane press. Explore the hilly red-clay of Georgia's Piedmont and learn about the inner-workings of this classic Southern cotton plantation. *gastateparks.org/jarrellplantation*, (478) 986-5172

Jarrell Plantation gives visitors a glimpse into the daily life on a Georgia plantation.

The historic buildings of downtown Macon are experiencing a revitilization.

Macon's extensive musical history is evident throughout the city.

Scenic Byways

While Georgia offers many reasons to visit and explore, the public transportation system is not one of them. With the exception of Atlanta, most cities in the state offer bus transportation on limited routes that would hinder your ability to explore and see some of the most interesting aspects of each location. So, you need a car to really appreciate the state, and once you are in that car you might want to incorporate a few scenic drives into your route. Fortunately, the state has established a scenic byway program that designates 15 distinct corridors for their historical, natural, recreational, cultural, and archeological significance. Oh, and they are pretty drives as well. The vast majority of these roads are off the beaten path, giving you a chance to exit the interstate and explore some of the roads-less traveled throughout the various regions of the state. If you

Scenic Byways can be found throughout the state.

really want to make it special, commit to stopping in some of the small towns to shop and dine in the locally-owned stores. There are plenty of excellent places throughout the state that aren't mentioned in this book, but all are well worth your time. Plus, it's always special to happen upon an undiscovered gem, knowing the vast majority of travelers never take the time to experience these hidden backroads and tucked away towns that were founded centuries ago. To help with planning your route, take a look at the scenic byways map found at dot.ga.gov/ds/travel/scenic.

MACON

Originally founded in 1823, Macon is undergoing a transformation that capitalizes on its historic downtown, located a short distance from the fast-moving Ocmulgee River. Perhaps one of the most noteworthy offerings in this city of 150,000 is the commitment to arts and culture, which stems from its rich musical heritage. This city is no one-trick pony, as there are many artists who have found success and achieved worldwide fame who can trace their humble beginnings in this city. Artists such as Little Richard, Otis Redding, the Allman Brothers, and Jason Aldean are all linked

to Macon, showcasing the star power the city has produced. There are plenty of local artists who would like to be the next superstar from central Georgia, too.

A revitalized downtown awaits the tens of thousands of visitors who pass through this city each and every year. Large events such as the **International Cherry Blossom Festival** (cherryblossom.com, 478-330-7050), **Just Tap'd Craft Beer Festival** (justtapdfestival.com, 478-599-9951), and the fantastic **Bragg Jam** (bragg jam.org) music festival all provide an opportunity for visitors to explore the city and appreciate its commitment

The Tubman Museum and Georgia Sports Hall of Fame are just a short stroll apart.

to culture. *maconga.org,* (478) 743-1074

THE HUMMINGBIRD STAGE & TAPROOM, MACON

For a truly authentic live music experience, check out this lively watering hole in the heart of downtown. Before bands make it big and start selling out stadiums, there's a good chance they roll through Macon and play a show on this stage, which has a formula that is part intimate, part dive bar, and many parts rockin'. *thebird stage.com,* (478) 741-9130

TUBMAN MUSEUM, MACON

This new 49,000-square-foot facility (the largest of its kind in the southeast) is located in the heart of downtown Macon. Although the name honors American icon Harriet

History and archaeology converge at Ocmulgee National Monument.

Tubman, the museum is much broader in scope. Inside the modern facility, visitors area greeted by a massive rotunda and multiple exhibitions that showcase African-American art, history, and culture. *tubmanmuseum .com, (478) 743-8544*

GEORGIA SPORTS HALL OF FAME, MACON

Honoring some of the greatest athletes who have played in the Peach State, this 43,000-square-foot facility offers exhibition space, thousands of artifacts, and interactive sports for visitors to try. Space is dedicated to history-making athletes from all levels, ranging from high school to the Olympics. There are also educational videos available that showcase the achievements of many famous athletes, including Herschel Walker. *georgiasportshalloffame.com, (478) 752-1585*

OCMULGEE NATIONAL MONUMENT, MACON

History and archaeology lovers will certainly enjoy a few hours at this site, which is managed by the National Park Service and covers over 17,000 years of human habitation. Visitors can watch a short film, examine more than 2,000 artifacts in the museum, and then take a stroll to the reconstructed Earth Lodge that dates back to 900 AD. If you want a bit of exercise, explore the multiple trails that wind throughout the 702-acre park. In 1933 the largest archaeological dig in American history occurred at this site, resulting in 2.5 million artifacts and an eye-opening look at the many civilizations that once lived here. *nps.gov/ocmu, (478) 752-8257*

HAY HOUSE, MACON

This exquisitely restored Italian Renaissance Revival home is a tour-de-force of antebellum architecture. Construction on this

If there is a better example of Renaissance Revival architecture, it will be hard to find.

18,000-square-foot mansion lasted four years and included a gorgeous two-story cupola on the roof. No expenses were spared during the design and construction, and it was one of the few homes at the time that had hot and cold water, central heat, and gas lighting. Take a tour of the home and gaze upon the detailed craftsmanship, as well as an excellent collection of art exhibited throughout the space. *hayhousemacon.org, (478) 742-8155*

THE ALLMAN BROTHERS BAND MUSEUM AT THE BIG HOUSE, MACON

One of the most iconic rock bands of all time recorded much of their work in Macon during the 1970s. The Allman Brothers initially formed in Jacksonville, Florida, but soon moved to Macon to be near their manager. It was here that they rose to fame and then tragically lost two members of

Allman Brothers fans will find much to love in the Big House Museum.

the band to separate motorcycle accidents. The Big House Museum has the largest collection of band memorabilia in the world and is filled with art, guitars, handwritten lyrics, and many personal belongings. *thebighousemuseum.com, (478) 741-5551*

SANDY BEACH PARK, MACON

Part beach, part water park, this recreational facility near Macon is a great way to cool off in the hot Georgia summer. Lay on the sandy white beach, go for a swim in Lake Tobesofkee, or enjoy the wide range of attractions inside the water park (the large waterslide is a favorite). Open Memorial Day through Labor Day. *maconwaterpark.net, (478) 477-5080*

MUSEUM OF AVIATION, WARNER ROBINS

Located on 51 acres near the Robins Air Force Base, this museum features a wide range of aircraft, from massive cargo planes to sleek fighters. Explore the four large buildings as well as the airplanes outside and you will gain an appreciation for the evolution of design and technology when it comes

Flannery O'Conner penned may of her famous works from this quaint farm outside of Milledgeville.

to military aircraft. Along with guided and self-guided tours, there is a specialized area for children. Best of all, it is free of charge. *museumofaviation .org, (478) 926-6870*

UNCLE REMUS MUSEUM, EATONTON

Several famous writers hail from central Georgia, including Alice Walker and Joel Chandler Harris. It was Harris who wrote the popular Uncle Remus stories that cemented him as one of the most influential writers in Georgia history. Uncle Remus was a fictional character who told colorful stories about Brer Rabbit in rural black dialect, reflecting the African-American folktales shared among slaves living in the South. This museum documents Harris's early life in Eatonton and the impact his writings had throughout the literary world. *uncleremusmuseum .org, (706) 485-6856*

ANDALUSIA, MILLEDGEVILLE

Visitors from all over the world come to visit this quaint farm located just

to the north of downtown Milledgeville. Author Flannery O'Conner lived here for 13 years and penned the majority of her masterpieces from the quiet solitude of the farmhouse, which now stands in stark contrast to the car dealerships and big box stores found just outside the gates. You can tour her home, take a stroll down to the pond, or visit with the peacocks she was so passionate about. *gcsu .edu/andalusia, (478) 445-8722*

GEORGIA'S OLD GOVERNOR'S MANSION, MILLEDGEVILLE

If you love history, antebellum architecture, or both, a visit to this mansion is well worth a few hours of your time. Located a short walk from bustling downtown, this place is steeped in history and is now an affiliate of the Smithsonian Institution. Thanks to generous funding in 2001, the mansion was immaculately restored to its former glory and today transports visitors back to its initial completion in 1839. Walk the halls, explore the

Georgia's Lake Country

Anchored by two lakes totaling almost 55 square miles, this area of Georgia offers activities for even the most discerning traveler. Both lakes were formed with dams constructed by Georgia Power, with only the Wallace Dam (near Milledgeville) separating the two large bodies of water. The result is a playground for children and adults, with activities that cater to all ages and incomes.

Lake Sinclair was formed by a large dam constructed back in 1954.

A boat rental is fun for the whole family.

There is plenty for the entire family on Lake Oconee.

Lake Oconee

A popular weekend destination for residents of the Atlanta area, Lake Oconee is surrounded by multimillion-dollar homes. In fact, a short boat ride will feel more like you are floating through an episode of *Lifestyles of the Rich and Famous,* because some of the mansions seem impossibly large. If you want a taste of what it's like to be rich and famous, get pampered at the **Ritz-Carlton** (ritzcarlton.com, 706-467-0600), which sits on the shores of the lake. Massages, golf, a day at the spa, or just lounging beside the exquisite pool can almost guarantee a day of relaxation.

For those who want to enjoy the refreshing water, there are plenty of ways to get out and explore. If you want a motor to do the work for you, rent a boat or jet ski from a wide range of providers. For those who want a more active role in the exploration, there are canoes, kayaks, paddleboards, and bicycles for rent. Check out **Young Harris Water Sports** (yhwatersports.com, 706-200-1720), **Oconee Wild Watersports** (oconeewildwatersports.com, 706-816-0166), and **Twin Lakes Jet Ski** (twinlakesjetski.com, 478-234-3446).

Downtown Greensboro has plenty of charm and is easily walkable.

If you are looking for a meal after, there are plenty of restaurants in the Lake Oconee area, but if you are looking for charm and authenticity head a short ways up the road to Greensboro. **The Yesterday Café** (theyesterdaycafe.com, 706-453-0800) is an unassuming little eatery that will take you back in time, giving you a glimpse of a Southern diner from the days when there were no computers or cell phones. The café is located in the heart of downtown and offers Southern classics at a reasonable price.

The placid waters of Georgia's Lake Country can be enjoyed year-round.

Lake Sinclair

Lake Sinclair sits directly to the south of Lake Oconee and offers many of the same activities as Oconee but with a slightly more relaxed vibe. It is a lake in transition, benefitting from the excessive home prices of Lake Oconee that force buyers to look elsewhere for their lakeside bungalows. The lake itself is quite large, touching three counties in central Georgia and providing some excellent bass fishing that brings sportsmen from near and far (there are tournaments frequently). With Milledgeville close by, a trip to Lake Sinclair offers a fun day on the water for those not seeking exclusivity and pampering.

The recently renovated **Sinclair Marina** (sinclairmarina.com, 478-451-0167) offers boat rentals and is just a short drive from downtown Milledgeville, giving you the opportunity to enjoy the lake and then grab a delicious meal afterward. If you want to eat where the locals go, check out **The Brick** (thebrick93.com, 478-452-0089). There's nothing fancy on the menu of pizza and pasta, but it is all good and reasonably priced. If carbs are your thing, the famous Stuffed Sticks won't disappoint.

Milledgeville has much to offer after a day out on the lake.

Whether you are on or off the water, there are several areas worth exploring in this part of Georgia. The two lakes are neighbored by several towns, including Greensboro, Eatonton, and Milledgeville. Each is separated by a 30-minute drive and offers antiques, gifts, dining, and a fair amount of history.

If you are looking for public access to the lakes, there are several locations that fit the bill. Lake Sinclair Recreation Area and Lawrence Shoals (on Lake Oconee) have camping, fishing, swimming, hiking, bathrooms, and picnic tables. Both locations give you a chance to enjoy the lakes if you don't want to rent a boat. *galakecountry.com*

The Old Governor's Mansion in Milledgeville offers architecture and history to the many visitors that walk inside.

rooms, and stand exactly where General Sherman did after he made the structure his headquarters in 1864. *gcsu.edu/mansion, (478) 445-4545*

WILDWOOD PARK, APPLING

Just outside of Augusta is a massive freshwater lake teeming with fish and other recreation possibilities. Part of the Savannah River basin, Clarks Hill is a reservoir that offers boating, swimming, hiking, biking, and abundant fishing. Wildwood Park offers easy access to the water and is also home to the International Disc Golf Center. For those unaware, disc golf is a very accessible sport that can be played by almost anyone. This could be a great location to play your first round. *(706) 541-0586*

AUGUSTA

Perhaps most famous for the annual Masters Golf Tournament that takes place in this city of 200,000, Augusta

has much more to offer than an ultra-exclusive golf course. The revitalized downtown sits on the banks of the substantial Savannah River, creating a rich setting for recreation with the convenience of nearby shopping and dining.

Founded in 1736 by General James Oglethorpe, the settlement was populated by traders who took advantage of the wide and free-flowing

Murals and other art installations can be found throughout downtown Augusta.

Georgia's Antebellum Trail

Before the Civil War began, the South was replete with areas of great prosperity. This Antebellum Era saw the rise of beautiful homes, massive plantations, a proliferation of towns and railroads to connect them, and even a gold rush. Though it has been several centuries since this period of time, plenty of remnants provide visitors with a glimpse into the architectural beauty and vivid history (both good and bad) of the years leading up to the Civil War. To make it easier for visitors to explore numerous destinations, museums, homes, and historical markers, an Antebellum Trail that stretches from Athens to Macon was created. Its website showcases an interactive map with plenty of ideas for the roughly 100-mile drive that includes seven cities. You will find beautifully restored homes, a quaint covered bridge, a battlefield, and plenty of antique stores as well. This could be a great way to transition from the mountains to the central part of the state, or vice versa. Regardless of the direction you travel in, you will traverse rolling hills, pastoral beauty, sleepy Southern towns, and larger urban areas that have transitioned into the twenty-first century without forgetting their roots. *antebellumtrail.org*

Thankfully, there is no shortage of antebellum homes in the state of Georgia.

Savannah River to move their wares down to the coast and beyond. The city played major roles in the Revolutionary War and then the Civil War, and is the location of President Woodrow Wilson's boyhood home, which can still be toured to this day.

Modern Augusta has seen a transformation in recent years, with new restaurants and retail establishments

The cathedral inside Sacred Heart is absolutely stunning.

opening along Broad Street, the main thoroughfare through downtown. The extensive free parking is a testament to just how visitor-friendly the downtown area is. This economic expansion has spread to neighboring streets as well, and a short walk around the downtown area highlights a rich and eclectic variety of shops. Art and culture make their mark almost everywhere, with several galleries

and public art installations throughout the downtown area for visitors to explore. Speaking of walking, the nearby Riverwalk offers excellent recreational opportunities along with expansive views across the Savannah River. The city offers plenty to fill your visit, and a few of the most popular locations are highlighted below. *Visit augusta.com, (706) 724-4067*

📷 SACRED HEART CULTURAL CENTER, AUGUSTA

Constructed in 1897 as a Catholic church, this building has been repurposed to exhibit art, history, and architecture. The exterior already commands attention, but step inside and you will be blown away by the craftsmanship and extensive renovations performed in the 1980s. Your eyes can't miss the stained glass windows, 94 of them in all. Come for the architecture and stick around for the art, as there are new exhibitions

> **DID YOU KNOW?** One of the most famous golf courses in the world is tucked away in the middle of Augusta. The Augusta National Golf Club is an ultra-exclusive course that hosts the annual Masters Tournament, drawing the best golfers in the sport. Since it first began in 1934, the tournament has been considered one of the most important every year and brings fans from around the world to walk the links with the pros.

The Augusta Canal 🌳

The Augusta Canal was built in 1846 with the purpose of providing water, power, and transportation to the city, and it continues to do all three of those things today. After its construction, a proliferation of cotton mills (eight in total) as well as lumber mills and other industries sprang up along its shores. Though initially designed for industry, the canal provided plenty of recreational opportunities for visitors, including a fifty-cent boat ride in the 1840s.

The canal is now a National Heritage Area managed by the National Park Service. Its head gates lie to the north of downtown, where water from the Savannah River flows into the artificial waterway. Also at the entrance to the canal sits **Savannah Rapids Park** (savannahrapids.com,

A dazzling sunset over downtown Augusta marks the end of another summer day.

706-868-3373), a beautiful recreation area that provides visitors with ample opportunities to get outside. A multi-use trail is an easy way for visitors to explore the canal and connects the park with downtown Augusta. Rent a bike, bring your own, or just take a leisurely stroll and snap some photos.

A cyclist explores the miles of paths that run along the canal.

A guided boat tour of the canal gives visitors a very different perspective.

If you want to get a little closer to the water, there are kayaks and canoes for rent. Speaking of close to the water, you can't beat the experience of stand-up paddleboarding (SUP) or windsurfing. Both activities have a learning curve, but fortunately **Whitecap Watersports** (whitecapsup.com, 706-833-9463) provides lessons for either. While this would be a very memorable way to explore the canal, there is no guarantee you'll stay dry. If you'd prefer a more leisurely tour, look no farther than **Petersburg Boat Tours** (augustacanal.com, 706-823-0440), which offers an open-air boat tour throughout the canal as a guide talks about the structures surrounding it, including textile mills, a Confederate gunpowder factory, and two homes constructed in the 1700s. After you disembark the vessel, head into their Canal Discovery Center to learn about the herculean task of excavating the canal in the mid 1800s.

The Morris Museum contains a wide range of artwork.

throughout the year, as well as musical performances. *sacredheart augusta.org, (706) 826-4700*

🖼 PHINIZY SWAMP NATURE PARK, AUGUSTA

If you want to get outside and explore the diverse beauty of a swamp while keeping your feet dry, this park is worth a visit. Miles of trails await, including elevated boardwalks that let you traverse the delicate environment while leaving no trace. Spanish moss, ospreys, beavers, croaking frogs, and an occasional alligator provide the setting for a day in the great outdoors. If you need to cool down, head inside and explore the natural history exhibit or the active bee colony that sits behind protective glass. *phinizy center.org, (706) 828-2109*

MORRIS MUSEUM OF ART, AUGUSTA

If you find yourself on the Riverwalk along the banks of the Savannah River, take some time to visit this beautiful museum, the oldest in the country devoted to the artists of the South. Inside the building you will find a permanent collection of more than 5,000 works and an ever-changing

DID YOU KNOW? The Godfather of Soul grew up in Augusta, overcoming the obstacles of the Great Depression and World War II to become a musical icon. James Brown was born in South Carolina but spent the majority of his formative years here.

James Brown is memorialized with a statue in the middle of downtown.

Dining in Augusta

A city like Augusta is guaranteed to have a variety of dining options, especially considering the influx of golfers, celebrities, and well-heeled spectators who descend on the area every year for the Masters.

The locals love **Whiskey Bar Kitchen** (whiskeybarkitchen.com, 706-814-6159), which offers excellent burgers, Japanese food, and a selection of whiskey that will make your head spin, perhaps even when you wake up the next morning. The atmosphere is lively and fun, making it a perfect downtown location to start (or end) your evening.

Whiskey Bar Kitchen lives up to its name, and then some.

If you'd rather spend a few hours in a quieter environment, **Frog Hollow Tavern** (froghollowtavern.com, 706-364-6906) offers an upscale dining experience with plenty of savory American cuisine on the menu.

For a laid-back dining experience that offers flavorful tapas, check out **The Bee's Knees** (beeskneestapas.com, 706-828-3600) in the heart of downtown. Along with tapas and a vegetarian-friendly menu, the cocktails are always on point.
If you're exploring downtown and just want to grab a quick bite, then you could do a lot worse than **Knuckle Sandwiches** (706-828-4700) on Broad Street. It's low-key and easy to miss, though the flavors are anything but.

space devoted to traveling exhibits. From abstract art to modern photography, there is plenty to satisfy your artistic curiosities. *themorris.org, (706) 724-7501*

PEXCHO DIME MUSEUM, AUGUSTA

In the 1800s, a dime would get you into museums that featured all kinds of oddities from across the globe. These "dime museums" were popular, probably because there was no Internet for gawking at all of the craziness. Fast forward to today, and you can look up almost anything you want, but if you want to see it up close and visit a place you might talk about with your friends for years to come, then stop in this peculiar shop just off Broad Street. You can grab a coffee and then proceed to take in all kinds of crazy exhibits, like two-headed mummies and alligator people. There's nowhere else like it in the United States, but it isn't for the faint of heart. *(706) 504-1291*

Agritourism

From its very inception one of the biggest industries in Georgia has been agriculture. Perhaps one of the best ways to learn about the state is through its farmland, vineyards, and stables that stretch from the mountains to the coast. There are a seemingly endless number of destinations from which to choose, ensuring that no matter where you are and where you are headed, you have some agricultural options awaiting you. While some of the destinations are for viewing and learning, others are much more hands-on. Options range from working dairy farms to picking your own peaches. If you'd rather be pampered, you can cozy up for a farm-to-table meal and then rest your head in a luxurious cabin for the night.

Sprawling fields and large tractors are a common sight across the Georgia countryside.

Even better, some of these locations are far removed from the interstate, giving you a great excuse to get off the beaten path and discover the scenic backroads, timeless small towns, and excellent mom-and-pop restaurants found throughout the state. If you plan to spend some time in the southern half of Georgia, you might be overwhelmed by the sheer number of agricultural destinations that exist. While normally all of these choices could create some confusion when planning your trip, fortunately there is a website that showcases many of the possible routes and visits throughout the region. **Georgia Grown Trails** (*georgiagrowntrails.com*) provides four possible routes that visitors can explore, connecting a variety of destinations in a way that facilitates an easy drive with plenty of options to enjoy.

DID YOU KNOW? In 1874, Georgia was the first state to establish a state Department of Agriculture.

MAGNOLIA SPRINGS STATE PARK, MILLEN

Crystal clear water, complete with a deep blue hue, flows from the earth in this remote park. Visitors find a blend of ecology, science, and history at a destination that is engaging and memorable. A boardwalk around the burbling springs affords visitors an excellent view of the cool water (72°F year-round), which bubbles to the surface from the Floridian aquifer located hundreds of feet below the ground. This water is a haven for animals, and it's not unusual to spot an alligator basking in the sun. After some time at the springs, head over to Camp Lawton, a Confederate prison that used to hold 10,000 Union soldiers. A nicely designed museum

Seven million gallons of fresh spring water flows to the surface every day.

provides context for the Civil War and the prison system, plus numerous artifacts. *gastateparks.org/Magnolia Springs, (478) 982-1660*

SPLASH IN THE BORO!, STATESBORO

It gets hot in Georgia, and if sand isn't your thing then this is a great spot to keep cool in the summer heat. Waterslides, a lazy river, a large wave pool, splash pads, and a flow rider ensure there is something for everyone. There are concessions on site and if you want some shade, opt for the cabana rental. Not too far down the road lies downtown Statesboro, which has plenty of bars and restaurants due to the presence of Georgia Southern University. *splashintheboro .com, (912) 489-3000*

A fun water park without the big crowds is part of the appeal.

SOUTH GEORGIA

South Georgia consists of the coastal plain, where oceans swept over the landscape during prehistoric times. While the water has long since receded, the sandy soil and relatively flat terrain serve as reminders that it was fish and marine life that originally inhabited this area, not the humans who have since settled the land. The region covers the majority of Georgia, roughly 35,650 square miles. Beginning at the Fall Line near the center of the state, the plain stretches all the way to the east coast where it meets the Atlantic Ocean. It is technically broken into two sections: the lower coastal plain and the upper coastal plain.

You'll find plenty of pine trees bordering expansive fields where farmers grow peanuts, cotton, pecans, blueberries, watermelons, and a whole host of other crops. Even if you have no map, you will know when you enter the southern part of the state. Exit the interstate, roll down a small highway, and marvel at the population density compared to the much more populous northern half of Georgia. Towns are fewer and farther between, and many of them have populations of 10,000 or fewer residents. While there are certainly some larger cities in this region, much of the charm can be found in these tiny communities that mostly look and feel the same as they did decades ago.

When you wander through the fields and pine forests of south Georgia, do yourself a favor and take your time. Stop for a while in

An old silo stands tall, though time has taken its toll on the exterior.

Plenty of cotton is still grown throughout the state of Georgia.

a tiny town and appreciate what life was like 50, 100, or 150 years ago when a train would stop at the station and provide a lifeline between the larger cities and these once bustling small towns that thrived on agricultural exports such as tobacco and cotton. Some towns are preserved, some are falling into disrepair, but many of the train depots still remain, along with the storefronts and stately buildings that served as the social and economic epicenters for the surrounding countryside. A trip by horse and carriage could take the better part of a day for a run to the grocery store, but it was a simpler time when people would stop for a conversation, a glass of sweet tea, and some respite from the hot sun of summer. Things weren't quite so hurried, the unending stream of information and social media didn't exist, and the never-ending farmland was the primary focus each and every day.

Sadly, too many of these small communities are just a shell of their previous selves, with a large number of residents long gone after the collapse of industry and agriculture that fueled the economic engine of the towns. Large highways and interstates now circumvent these quaint downtown areas, depriving the mom-and-pop stores of needed tourist income. At the end of the day, you might save 20 minutes taking the interstate on this part of your journey, but you miss out on a slice of history and a large swath of the state that provides fantastic insight into the true essence of Georgia.

Pecan orchards are common in the central and southern part of the state.

Big thunderstorms are common throughout the summer months.

Libations in South Georgia

Albany
Pretoria Fields Collective
pretoriafields.com

Arlington
Still Pond Vineyard and Winery
stillpond.com

Bainbridge
Southern Philosophy Brewing
southernphilosophybrewing.com

Boston
Buzzery Pizza & Mead
thebuzzery.com

Byron
Cane River Winery
caneriverwinery144.wixsite.com

Watermelon Creek Vineyard
watermeloncreekvineyard.com

Hartsfield
Gin Creek Vineyards and Winery
gincreek.com

Kathleen
Tilford Winery
tilfordwinery.com

Mauk
Five Points Berries
fivepointsberries.com

Nashville
Horse Creek Winery at Perry Vineyards
horsecreekwinery.com

Pelham
Farmer's Daughter Vineyards
farmersdaughtervineyards.com

Valdosta
Georgia Beer Co.
georgiabeerco.com

Wray
Paulk Vineyards
paulkvineyards.com

PROVIDENCE CANYON STATE PARK, LUMPKIN

Commonly referred to as Georgia's "Little Grand Canyon," this formation is man-made, but not in the traditional sense of the term. Due to poor farming practices in the 1800s, soil erosion occurred at an increasingly alarming rate, and the soft, sandy soil of the region began to wash away, forming gullies that deepened after every passing storm. The result is a paradoxically beautiful network of canyons and chasms that stretch throughout the 1,109-acre state recreation area. Visitors can enjoy views from several vantage points around the rim of the canyon, or take a moderate hike down to the canyon floor for further exploration. The canyon is forever changing due to the sandy soil and relatively rapid erosion, sometimes widening by a foot or more per year. As you hike through the network of trails on the canyon floor, you no longer feel as if you are in Georgia (or anywhere else in the southeast). Walls stretch to the sky and trees sprout from precarious ledges, their roots clinging to the soft soil. The park itself has no accommodations and only a small handful of primitive campsites, but the unique beauty of the area makes this a must-visit for anyone in the area. *gastate parks.org/ProvidenceCanyon, (229) 864-7275*

The sun rises over the geologic beauty of Providence Canyon.

The sandy soil of Providence Canyon erodes rapidly in heavy rains.

Georgia's President

While politics can be divisive and you will always get a range of opinions when discussing a president, few can debate the humanitarian contributions that President Jimmy Carter has made since his time as the nation's 39th president. Hailing from the small town of Plains, this peanut farmer became governor of Georgia before running and winning the US presidency in 1976. After losing to Ronald Reagan in 1980, Carter returned to Plains and began several humanitarian initiatives that would cement his legacy as one of compassion, kindness, and grace. Thanks to his extensive work with Habitat for Humanity, as well as his unending efforts to promote human rights and peaceful solutions to conflict, Carter won the Nobel Peace Prize in 2002. His focus on spirituality is apparent to all who have attended his Sunday school classes at Maranatha Baptist Church in Plains. Open to the public, it isn't uncommon for visitors from around the world to start lining up on Saturday night for the Sunday morning service.

President Carter sits in the sanctuary of his church.

PLAINS

"Peanuts and a President" should be the unofficial slogan of this tiny town in rural Georgia. With a population of under one thousand, this town's claim to fame is President Jimmy Carter, who still lives here and regularly teaches Sunday school at Maranatha Baptist Church (the general public is welcome, although space is limited). If you really want to learn more about the 39th President of the United States, you can visit his boyhood farm, the 1888 train depot (site of his presidential campaign headquarters), and the museum at

The old train depot served as President Carter's campaign headquarters.

Plains High School. The small size of Plains ensures easy access and travel to the various locations, making this trip educational and efficient. Plains isn't only about Carter, though; it also attracts thousands of people to its annual Peanut Festival, which celebrates the ubiquitous legume that is harvested extensively in the region. *plainsgeorgia2.com, (229) 824-5373*

WINDSOR HOTEL, AMERICUS

It takes a special hotel to be featured in this book, and that is exactly what you can call this historical icon. Constructed in the late 1800s to attract affluent Northerners during the wintertime, this architectural masterpiece is a showcase in Victorian

The architecure of the Windsor Hotel has been faithfully preserved over the past century.

design. A stunning open lobby with intricate woodwork and soaring ceilings greet you when you walk inside. You are truly stepping into history, as the building has been frequented by a range of celebrities and politicians. Tales of haunted hallways add to the mystique of the location, and if you don't have a chance to stay the night you should at least step inside. *windsor-americus.com, (229) 924-1555*

ANDERSONVILLE NATIONAL HISTORIC SITE, ANDERSONVILLE

The Civil War was one of the darkest times in our nation's history, and Andersonville is a historical reminder of just how awful war can be. Known officially as Camp Sumter, this prison housed more than 45,000 Union soldiers over the course of a year, with over a quarter of them dying from disease or terrible environmental conditions. The misery and suffering that occurred here is a solemn reminder of the horrors of war, contrasting strongly with the natural beauty visitors will now find when they arrive. You can walk the grounds and get a glimpse of the overall scale of the prison, including a reconstructed stockade. A free, self-guided audio tour is available to all visitors, and after your outside tour you can step into the National Prisoner of War Museum, which provides insight into prisoners of war throughout American History. The Andersonville National Cemetery is also found here, serving as the final resting place for almost 20,000 individuals. *nps.gov/ande, (229) 924-0343*

RADIUM SPRINGS, ALBANY

Not far from downtown Albany lies a spring that pumps out more than 70,000 gallons of cool water every

Peaceful and solemn, the cemetery at Andersonville is a visual reminder of the cost of war.

minute of the day, resulting in a beautiful blue hue and refreshing environment for plants and animals. These springs are so unique they have been designated one of the Seven Natural Wonders of Georgia. Once a resort known as the Casino, the springs have seen dinners, dances, beauty pageants, and plenty of bathers relaxing in the water that feeds the nearby Flint River. Swimming is no longer allowed, but you can still appreciate the history and peacefulness that exists throughout the grounds.

CHEHAW PARK, ALBANY

Remarkably, there are only two accredited zoos in Georgia, and this is one of them. Located on 700 acres

Quail

If you know anything about quail hunting, then you already know that southwest Georgia is the quail hunting capital of the world. Visitors from all over the globe travel here because of the expansive land, agreeable weather, and abundance of birds. Every September through March, hunters descend on the area with their shotguns, resting their heads every night in a variety of lodges that cater to the well-heeled from Beverly Hills and Wall Street. You don't have to be particularly wealthy to hunt these birds, but it certainly helps. Many of these plantations provide everything you need during your stay, including a dog, usually an English Pointer, bred to flush the winged creatures out of the brush. Typically you will pay a fixed amount for each bird you take, and there are usually other amenities available, such as a comfortable cabin, excellent meals, a well-stocked bar, and a pool table at which to challenge your friends. If you want to splurge and experience this aristocratic sport, check out popular destinations such as the **Wynfield Plantation** (wynfieldplantation.com, 229-889-0193) in Albany or the **Riverview Plantation** (riverviewplantation.com, 229-294-4904) near Camilla. The northern part of the state also offers opportunities, including the **South Fork Hunting Preserve** (southforkhunting preserve.com, 706-255-9524) near Danielsville.

Quail hunting brings people to Georgia from across the US and around the world.

in the southwest part of the state, this zoo places a strong focus on nature conservation. Not only can you enjoy an up-close look at more than 238 species of animals, including cheetahs, bobcats, zebras, and bald eagles, but there are plenty of recreational opportunities as well.

A BMX track, splash pad, mountain bike trails, and a nice campground all contribute to making this a memorable experience for the entire family. *chehaw.org, (229) 430-5275*

FLINT RIVERQUARIUM, ALBANY

The most populous city in southwest Georgia is home to a surprisingly large aquarium that features aquatic life from Georgia and beyond. The 54,000-square-foot facility is located on the banks of the Flint River, which begins under (yes, under) the Atlanta airport and flows south, eventually joining the Chattahoochee before emptying into the Gulf of Mexico. Visitors are treated to numerous exhibits that highlight the Flint River basin,

The RiverQuarium in downtown Albany offers many educational exhibits.

including a 175,000-gallon tank that is naturally filled by a blue hole spring underneath. An albino alligator, octopus, numerous turtles, and huge sturgeon are just a few of the creatures you will see during your visit. *flintriver quarium.com, (229) 639-2650*

KOLOMOKI MOUNDS STATE PARK, BLAKELY

The oldest and largest Woodland Indian site in the southeastern United States offers plenty of history along with hiking trails, a sandy beach, miniature golf, and even paddle boats. Exploring the ceremonial mounds will provide some education and a bit of physical activity. There is a museum full of artifacts along with a full campground at the park. *gastate parks.org/kolomokimounds, (229) 724-2150*

SWAMP GRAVY, COLQUITT

If you enjoy the arts, live entertainment, and the rural South, prepare to be amazed by this long-running performance that brings storytelling to life on a stage in the small town of Colquitt. An unpretentious red brick building in the middle of downtown is the home of Cotton Hall Theater, where more than one hundred volunteers bring true stories of life in rural Georgia to the stage with a blend of song, dance, and plenty of laughter. The juxtaposition of this tiny town and the state-of-the-art lighting and set design that you'll find inside the theater is almost worth the trip by itself, but it's the performances that have led to its regional and even national acclaim. The original show is now performed in October and March, with other productions filling out the rest of the entertainment calendar. *swampgravy.com, (229) 758-5450*

The lights of downtown Thomasville cast a warm glow after the sun sets in the distance.

THOMASVILLE

Seemingly in the middle of nowhere (but really only a half an hour north of Tallahassee) is this small, beautiful, lively town full of shopping, dining, art, and history. When you arrive downtown, you are greeted by the rhythmic thump of your tires rolling over the red brick streets, which were laid in 1907. An interesting anecdote––the bricks were manufactured by the Augusta Brick Company and one side of each brick bore the word *Augusta*. Workers originally laid the bricks with the word clearly visible, but the mayor was having none of it. The bricks were dug up, flipped over, and reset, but a few were overlooked and can still be spotted if you have a watchful eye. There is much to love about this small town that positively oozes Southern charm. Palm trees and live oaks abound, making it feel almost Savannah-esque. *thomasvillega.com, (229) 227-7020*

GRASSROOTS COFFEE, THOMASVILLE

If you need some caffeine and perhaps a place to check your email, this inviting coffee shop in the center of downtown has you covered. They roast their own beans at a warehouse in town, ensuring a perfect cup of coffee to go along with a variety of fresh food and pastries on their menu. This is a great place to rest your feet and plan your day's adventures in and around Thomasville. *grassrootscoffee .com, (229) 226-3388*

BIG OAK, THOMASVILLE

Thomasville is a very walkable town, so go out and stroll the streets, check out the wide array of locally-owned shops, and then head a few blocks north to appreciate the famous Big Oak. This historical landmark is absolutely magnificent, with a trunk circumference of almost 27 feet and limbs that span over 165 feet. The

Passing cars rumble over the bricks throughout downtown.

A watertower is framed by a live oak in the middle of downtown.

tree dates back to 1680, making it one of the oldest live oaks east of the Mississippi. The tree sits in the middle of a neighborhood, so from here you can take a stroll to marvel at the numerous historic homes that stretch in every direction. Considering the history of the city, it's no wonder there are so many impressive homes.

LAPHAM-PATTERSON HOUSE, THOMASVILLE

Founded in 1825, the City of Roses (rose bushes abound) became the winter destination for wealthy Northerners near the turn of the twentieth century. The climate, availability of land, and easy access via railroad helped contribute to its rise.

One of the oldest live oaks east of the Mississippi resides in Thomasville.

Highly unique architecture is a hallmark of the Lapham-Patterson house.

The expansive Pebble Hill Plantation is open to the public.

The result—large beautiful homes and massive plantations were constructed and remain to this day. Perhaps one of the finest examples of Victorian-era architecture is the **Lapham-Patterson House** (gastate parks.org/LaphamPattersonHouse, 229-226-7664), which is part of the Georgia State Parks system but managed by the Thomasville History Center. The winter "cottage" for Chicago shoe merchant C.W. Lapham, this 6,000-square-foot home showcases many unique design features, enough for it to eventually be designated as a National Historic Landmark.

📷 PEBBLE HILL PLANTATION, THOMASVILLE

If you love history, visit this beautifully-preserved house and plantation a short drive from downtown Thomasville. This sprawling 3,000-acre property was originally a working farm but was later converted into a shooting plantation in the late 1800s. It features numerous buildings, a large stable with horses, and the 26,000-square-foot main home,

complete with an art gallery. Stroll the manicured grounds and explore the original buildings scattered throughout the property—there is even a dog hospital. Once in the main home, you will be struck by the attention to detail, the craftsmanship, and the commitment to preservation. Everything is original, and no words can truly capture the experience. *pebblehill.com, (229) 226-2344*

🦬 SEMINOLE STATE PARK, DONALSONVILLE

A sandy beach, hiking trails, and easy access to a fisherman's paradise make this state park popular among people in southwest Georgia and beyond. You'll spot plenty of wildlife as you walk along the lake, or you can paddle out into the water to get up close with everything from bald eagles to alligators. On-site canoe and kayak rentals make it easy to spend time out on the water for an hour or even a day, then relax in a cottage and watch the sun drop over the 37,000-acre lake. *gastateparks.org/seminole, (229) 861-3137*

Dining in Thomasville

Exploring all the fascinating offerings of Thomasville might get your appetite going, but fortunately there are plenty of restaurants to quell that problem. If you ask any of the locals where to eat, they will probably tell you **Jonah's Fish and Grits** (jonahsfish.com, 229-226-0508) or **Sweet Grass Dairy** (sweetgrassdairy.com, 229-228-6704). Jonah's is predominantly seafood, and if you like shrimp and grits this might be the best bowl you ever eat (the accompanying hush puppy is equally superb). At Sweet Grass you will be treated with a vast selection of homemade cheese (it's so good they ship it all over the world), along with charcuterie, salads, and sandwiches. If you can swing it, do lunch at Sweet Grass and dinner at Jonah's.

GEORGIA MUSEUM OF AGRICULTURE AND HISTORIC VILLAGE, TIFTON

Managed by Abraham Baldwin Agricultural College, this interactive museum gives visitors an insightful look at the backbone of Georgia's history: agriculture. In the nineteenth century, farmers sweltered in the south Georgia heat (hard to imagine without air conditioning) to plant and harvest a wide range of crops. This history comes alive every day within the village as the staff performs activities in a sawmill, blacksmith's shop, or grist mill. A beautiful Victorian home is available to tour, along with another 35 structures that have been relocated to these 95 acres just outside of Tifton. *gma.abac.edu, (229) 391-5205*

BANKS LAKE NATIONAL WILDLIFE REFUGE, LAKELAND

Over 4,000 acres of freshwater lakes and marsh provide a fertile breeding ground for a large variety of fish and wildlife. The striking cypress trees create a picturesque setting for those wanting to get out on the water and dip a line, or take a relaxing paddle through the lake and waterways. While there is a short walking trail for those who want to explore

The Georgia Museum of Agriculture gives visitors a glimpse into the past.

the shoreline, your best bet is to rent a kayak (there are plenty available onsite) and get out onto the water.

Fishing

Georgia is an outdoor lover's paradise, with many options for those who love to hike, camp, fish, and hunt. The vast array of streams and lakes are fertile grounds for fish of all kinds. Couple that with the marsh and Atlantic Ocean and practically every angler will be satisfied. Of course you'll need a fishing license, which costs $10 a day for non-residents (or $50 annually) and $15 annually for residents.

Starting at the coast, there is an abundance of options for catching a variety of fish, including redfish, snapper, and tarpon. From piers on the marsh to miles of sand on the Atlantic, all you need is a rod, reel, some bait, and maybe a chair to sit in. While it's possible to catch something large from the shore, your chances are greatly increased if you head out into deeper water on a boat. There are charter operations all along the coast, but the popularity of Saint Simon's Island brings with it some excellent options. If you have children or an avid angler in your group, try **Island Lure Charters** (fishthegoldenisles.com, 912-266-7167), which specializes in a variety of trips to locations all over the Georgia coast. Reeling in a 100 blacktip shark will definitely provide a lasting memory!

Lakes and rivers throughout the state provide even more opportunities for anglers. If you like the idea of landing a bass, you are in luck! There are 32 large lakes full of them. Public access is available on all of Georgia's lakes, with docks and piers that provide access to deeper water and more fish. You can certainly catch a fish on almost any lake or river in the state, but some of the standouts include **Clark's Hill** (a 55-pound striped bass has been caught here), **Lake Sinclair**, and **Lake Seminole** down near the Florida line. The warmer weather of south Georgia makes this lake a great option in the colder months. Depending on the location, a variety of live bait and artificial lures can be used for a memorable outing. There are also boat rentals available on almost every lake in the state, facilitating access to the deepest water and hidden coves.

One relatively unique offering in Georgia is the trout that inhabit the waters of the Georgia mountains. These fish can be caught with a traditional rod and reel, but the art of fly fishing is common within the streams that flow through the mountains and down toward the Atlantic. Every year, the streams are stocked with a selection of rainbow,

You can't beat the ease of fishing from shore along the Georgia coast.

Bass fishing is very popular throughout the lakes of Georgia.

Fly fishing is an art form, but practice can pay off in a big way.

brown, and brook trout to meet the needs of anglers who come from all over the country. Over 4,000 miles of streams flow through the Georgia mountains, so it might be hard to choose where you want to fish. Some of the top streams include the **Toccoa River**, the **Chattahoochee River**, **Rock Creek**, and the **Chattooga**. Anglers can find good information about public access to these rivers on the Georgia Outdoor Network website (gon.com), but if you want the best chance to catch a nice trout (and work on your casting), you might be smart to hire a professional. One of the most well-known fly fishing shops in the state is **Unicoi Oufitters** (unicoioutfitters.com, 706-878-3083) based out of Helen. The shop offers guided excursions on multiple streams and rivers, as well as a beginner's class that brings you up to speed no matter what your age or ability.

fws.gov/refugre/banks_lake, (912) 496-7836

VALDOSTA

Millions of people pass Valdosta each year as it sits on Interstate 75 just a short distance from the Florida line. It is the largest city in south Georgia and is home to Valdosta State University, which contributes to the young vibe felt throughout downtown and beyond. The city of 56,000 has a nice blend of food, culture, art, and a bit of excitement as well. *visitvaldosta.org*, *(229) 559-5828*

While events at the university bring a lot of people to the area, one of the biggest, and most visible, attractions in Valdosta is **Wild Adventures Theme Park** (wildadventures.com, 229-219-7080), which offers rides, a waterpark, a zoo, a live concert series, and a discovery center dedicated to adventure-filled exploration for children of all ages. Nowhere else can you feed a giraffe, get inverted on a shuttle coaster, hurdle down a waterslide, and then enjoy the tranquility of a butterfly garden, all within the same park. A massive dinosaur park features 20 life-sized dinosaurs to marvel at, and a summer

concert series brings in major headliners spanning musical genres. There are literally days of activities available for visitors of all ages, so plan accordingly.

If crowds of people aren't your thing, then go get lost in in the **Grand Bay Wildlife Management Area,** which encompasses thousands of acres of forest and wetlands. Elevated boardwalks and hiking trails allow visitors to explore the natural surroundings while an education center provides an interpretive experience of the immense wetlands that constitute Grand Bay.

Working up an appetite in Valdosta isn't a bad thing, because there are some excellent places to grab a bite to eat. Lovers of Southern cuisine will enjoy **Steel Magnolias** (steelmagnoliasvaldosta.com, 229-259-0010), a restaurant that specializes in cooking up Southern classics with a more modern flair. Sit on the rooftop, sip on a drink, and order some food off of the extensive and constantly changing menu. If you're looking for something a bit more casual and won't find yourself near the coast anytime soon, you can get some great seafood at **Bubba Jax Crab Shack** (229-469-4368). The glorified shack has just the necessities—a place to sit and food that will leave you satisfied.

WAYCROSS

Across the plains of south Georgia, visitors find unending agriculture interrupted by occasional urban development. One of the (relatively) larger cities is Waycross, with a population of roughly 15,000 residents. It sits just north of the Okefenokee Swamp, serving as a convenient post from which to make a day trip down to the swamp and still return to the

owntown Valdosta offers plenty of shopping,
ning, and entertainment.

Grand Bay Wildlife Management is a nice place
for a stroll.

Vild Adventures offers something for everyone in the family.

Paddling Georgia

Georgia has a wide variety of rivers, from crystal clear rapids that cascade through the higher elevations, to the dark and nutrient-rich blackwater that fills the swamps of the southern end of the state. There are 70,150 miles of rivers that traverse Georgia, with 14 major river basins and 52 different watersheds. All this water means one thing to adventure lovers—paddling. There is no better way to explore a waterway than under your own power, be it in a canoe, kayak, or larger inflatable. The quiet solitude, the symphony of nature, and the burbling of the water as it searches for the least resistance on its journey to the ocean all create an atmosphere of quiet reflection and enjoyment. You can, of course, do it alone, as there are plenty of rivers and rental companies across the state. But for some, it is safest and most convenient to find a guide or an event to help with the logistics. If you want to see miles and miles of the state that are inaccessible by road, then head over to the **Georgia River Network** (garivers.org, 706-549-4508) to learn about the numerous trips planned throughout the state every year.

One of the premier events is the annual Paddle Georgia gathering, also one of the largest paddling events in the United States. Each summer, participants spend seven days paddling and floating down one or more of the many rivers that flow throughout the state. The trip takes paddlers of all skill levels on a journey down one of the main rivers of the state, complete with nightly camping, catered meals, and a large group of like-minded people. The group size is typically more than 200 people, with 10 to 15 miles of paddling per day. The paddling is always with the current of the river, ensuring

Paddling the estuaries of Georgia's coast is a great way to explore hidden locations.

The scenic Altamaha brings you through remote areas that are packed with history.

that people with varying physical abilities can enjoy the adventure. While the event is open to anyone, participants need to have some basic experience in a canoe or kayak. If you don't have your own boat, there are rentals available.

If you aren't looking for something organized and would rather head out on your own, there are plenty of locations throughout the state to do so. One of the most uniquely beautiful rivers is the Altamaha, the third-largest watershed in the eastern United States, which winds its way through some truly isolated and wild landscape before flowing into the Atlantic Ocean north of Brunswick. Along the way paddlers are greeted by undisturbed forest, expansive marshes, and animal species that call the river basin home. If you don't have your own equipment, stop by **Three Rivers Outdoors** (3riversoutdoor.com, 912-594-8379) in the small town of Uvalda and they will hook you up with everything you need. The shop is located directly on the Altamaha River and offers guided trips as well.

Large alligators are very common throughout the park and beyond.

The Korean War memorial is a centerpiece in downtown Waycross.

creature comforts of modern society at the end of your adventure.

The **Okefenokee Swamp Park** (*okeswamp.com, 912-283-0583*) sits at the northern edge of the vast wilderness area, only 13 miles from the downtown area. After paying for admission, visitors have easy access to the swamp through boat tours or a short railroad, and can also explore the interpretive nature exhibits that look at the flora and fauna that is so prevalent throughout the swamp.

If you are looking for a bite to eat, try **KD's Café** (kdscafe.com, 912-285-3300) in the middle of downtown. A menu with variety and excellent service should leave you satisfied. *Way crosstourism.com, (912) 287-2969*

STEPHEN C. FOSTER STATE PARK, FARGO

A remote gateway to the spectacular Okefenokee Swamp, this state park is almost 20 miles from civilization, in the tiny town of Fargo. Keep this in mind when you plan your visit, as you will want to bring all of your food and supplies with you. Visitors will find camping, cabins, and easy access to the western side of the swamp. There are daily boat tours available, or you can rent a kayak and start paddling. Word to the wise though: Don't approach the alligators (the population is estimated at over 12,000), as many will be larger than your boat. *gastateparks.org/stephencfoster, (912) 637-5274*

Okefenokee Swamp 📷 🌳

This massive, 402,000-acre swamp is one of Georgia's Seven Natural Wonders, and for good reason. The swamp is so large—and so unexplored—that large swaths of it have never been touched by mankind. It is perhaps the most isolated location in the entire state, and the lack of human civilization means it is Dark-Sky certified by the International Dark-Sky Association, one of only a handful of such places in the southeast. This translates into spectacular views of the stars and Milky Way, and a complete haven for astrophotographers.

Night skies aside, the main draw to the swamp is the rich ecosystem, with well over 12,000 alligators, 620 species of plants, 234 species of birds, almost 80 species of fish and amphibians, and 50 species of mammals, including black bears. It is certainly one of the most ecologically diverse locations in this part of the United States. While the numerous alligators are some of the most visible and exciting creatures, it is an ideal location for bird lovers as well. There are several open waterways that afford long range views of the many avian species that reside within this National Wildlife Refuge.

The history behind this blackwater swamp—the largest in the United States—is an intriguing one. So harsh are the living conditions among the 70 islands that it is hard to imagine why people would occupy it. But the natural resources, in addition to the ability to get lost and stay lost, has long attracted mankind to the area. Evidence in the park suggests that there have been at least two major Native American occupations, one beginning in A.D. 500 and another in A.D. 1200. Sand mounds and other artifacts are still visible in the swamp to this day, with several present on Floyd's Island. Sadly, like in many other areas in the United States, the Native Americans were displaced by settlers looking for land and industry. The bugs, snakes, alligators, bears, and disease were all factors against inhabiting this area, but there was one natural resource that lured settlers despite the conditions: timber. Thick, dense forest provided ample opportunities for logging operations, and the ubiquitous cypress trees were particularly valuable. A railroad was built from Waycross to Billy's Island, facilitating the removal of the trees once they were harvested. The railroad ushered in a slew of workers who needed housing and entertainment. A movie theater, doctor's offices, churches, company store, icehouse, and schools were all constructed. The cypress trees were cut, milled, and hauled away by the railroad, scarring the earth and altering the ecosystem that is home to so

Baby alligators sun themselves on a log in the Okefenokee.

The bird watching within the Okefenokee is excellent.

Narrow waterways and Spanish moss are pervasive throughout the swamp.

many different plants and animals. The logging eventually ceased, but you can still visit the island and wander through the remnants of the old town.

Like many other ecological areas, the swamp is at the mercy of the weather and ever-changing climate. Long periods of drought have occurred, making navigation difficult or nearly impossible. More concerning is the susceptibility for fire, since most of the swamp is unreachable and cannot be easily managed like other parks and natural areas. The Honey Prairie Fire of 2011 is an example of just how bad things can get, when a bolt of lightning started a fire that burned for almost an entire year and consumed nearly 75 percent of the refuge. The swamp has since recovered from this massive fire, although charred tree stumps and open prairies stand as reminders of how quickly a landscape can change. *fws.gov/refuge/okefenokee, (912) 496-7836*

The sunrise casts a pink hue on Cumberland Island.

COASTAL GEORGIA

Just as many people don't realize the scope and beauty of the Appalachians in north Georgia, others may not be aware of the natural splendor along the one hundred miles of Georgia's Atlantic coastline. Countless islands lie within the marsh and are subject to the daily tides that give, and take, access to the sea. The appeal of the Georgia coast isn't just the beaches and weathered trees that can tell stories about Native Americans and British colonists; it's the variety and scale of each plot of land that sits just high enough above the Atlantic to not be submerged by the daily tides. These islands, which range tremendously in size and population, offer something for everyone. Locations along the coast provide possibilities no matter what your budget and priorities, from luxury hotels and high-end retail establishments, to solitude and environmental grandeur that is seemingly undisturbed by mankind.

Looking for where the Atlanta upper class go on their beach vacations? Check out **Sea Island** with its immaculate resort and manicured golf course. Ultra-exclusive and only for the well-heeled, you will be coddled and pampered for the entirety of your stay.

Winding creeks flow through the estuaries of coastal Georgia.

The Milky Way lights up the night sky over Driftwood Beach.

For a blend of fancy and laid back, hop across the marsh to **Saint Simons Island,** which caters to a range of travelers and budgets. Expensive homes and beautiful neighborhoods surround the charming downtown, which sits on the water and provides all of the food, shopping, and entertainment a beachgoer could hope for.

Jekyll Island is beloved by almost everyone for its mix of old island homes, modest hotels, and secluded pathways that thread throughout the island. It is laid out to be explored by foot or bicycle, minimizing the noise pollution of cars and maximizing the enjoyment of the nature lovers who flock to its shores throughout the year.

Want to get away from people? Check out the fascinating history and empty beaches of **Sapelo Island**. *Really* want to get away from people? **Cumberland Island** ticks all of the boxes, and there is a distinct possibility you might see more wild horses than humans during your stay.

The Georgia coast doesn't have the sugar white sand of the Florida Gulf, but it has gnarled driftwood, infatuating tides, thousands of small waterways to explore, and a variety of islands with strong identities. Their close proximity to each other means you don't have to settle on just one—you can explore the entire coast in a few days or a few weeks, depending on how much time you would like to relax and soak it all in. So grab your flip-flops, a beach towel, and some sunscreen, take a look at the map, and start plotting your course. If you have the time, start in Savannah and work your way south to the Florida line, hitting the sand, the history, the art, and the culinary brilliance that emanates from each of these treasures. No matter where you are along the shores of the Atlantic, you can watch the sun rise over the ocean and set over the marsh, because the coast isn't a defined line. It is a mesh of islands, waterways, estuaries, and the swirling ocean. It is unmistakably Georgia.

The warmth of the rising sun sweeps over the live oak trees.

Libations in Coastal Georgia

Brunswick
Hop Soul Brewery
hopsoulbrewery.com

Silver Bluff Brewing Company
silverbluff.com

Savannah
Coastal Empire Brewing
coastalempirebeer.com

Moon River
moonriverbrewing.com

Service Brewing Co.
servicebrewing.com

Southbound
southboundbrewingco.com

Two Tides Brewing
twotidesbrewing.com

Saint Marys
Brackish Beer Co.
(912) 322-6743

SAVANNAH

Gas lamps, cobblestone streets, Spanish moss lazily swaying in the breeze—this is Savannah, a magical place that lives up to and far exceeds its worldwide reputation. It is a place of mystery, history, and Southern charm that permeates the city. Art is everywhere, as is music, and you are all but guaranteed to eat some excellent food during your stay. Its close proximity to the Atlantic means plenty of fresh seafood, as well as recreational opportunities. Tales of ghosts and haunted homes are rampant—Savannah is considered one of the most haunted cities in America. Practically an entire day can be spent lounging about in the 22 squares found throughout the historic district, squares that serve as gathering places for residents, college students, and visitors alike. Perhaps the most famous is **Chippewa Square,** the setting for the bus stop scene in *Forrest Gump*. It will likely be crowded with visitors snapping photos, but feel free to take refuge in one of the other equally beautiful greenspaces lined with live oaks (which serve as the official state tree of Georgia). The fast-moving Savannah River provides access for impossibly large cargo ships, many destined for Europe, Africa, and beyond. There is much to do and experience in this city, and the slow pace of life can be addictive. If you have time, dedicate several days to this cultural paradise so you can relax, explore, and truly appreciate the Savannah experience.

DID YOU KNOW? A highly skilled mechanic and inventor named Eli Whitney invented the first cotton gin at Mulberry Grove plantation, located just outside Savannah.

Settled in 1733 by General James Oglethorpe, Savannah was the first established city in the 13th colony of Georgia. The city was the first in the United States designed and planned from the outset, with 24 original squares established throughout the city in a consistent pattern. The

The sun rises over the historic district in downtown Savannah.

Large boats provide a memorable setting for River Street.

squares were intended to be places for people to meet and congregate, and that continues to this day. The massive and ubiquitous live oak trees provide shade from the hot Georgia sun, and lush grass offers a carpet-like surface on which to relax, have a picnic, read a book, or take a nap.

An artist finds inspiration in one of the many squares in Savannah.

Most of the downtown sits on a bluff, protecting the buildings from unforeseen floods and providing a nice vantage point for views of the river and distant landscape. Unfortunately, the bluff does nothing to combat fire, and the city was decimated by large fires in 1796 and again in 1820. Further adding to the misery of its residents, a yellow fever outbreak in 1820 killed more than 10 percent of the population. Savannah was the source of naval blockades in the Civil War, which slowed the local economy to a crawl, putting many out of work and thrusting families into poverty. It was the final destination of Sherman's destructive March to the Sea, but the city was so beautiful that Sherman couldn't burn it. Instead he gifted it to President Lincoln at Christmas.

It's the little things that make you fall in love with this place. The unmistakable rhythmic sound of horses walking across the cobblestone streets, a sound that harks back to the early days when there were no cars motoring past. A warm breeze that sways the limbs of the live oaks. A peaceful night stroll on a quiet street, and the dim flickering light of gas lamps outside some of the oldest homes in Georgia. It's the excellent shopping on Broughton Street, filled with retail stores for all tastes and budgets. It's the occasional peak you get into the backyards throughout the historic district, small oases full of vibrant green plants and burbling fountains. It's the slow and steady progress of a ship as it heads to sea, or the silent strokes of an artist's brush in Chatham Square. This is Savannah, and it beckons for a piece of your heart. *visitsavannah.com,* *(912) 644-6400*

DID YOU KNOW? The cobblestones found in many of Savannah's streets come from the far reaches of the globe, as they were originally used as ballast on the merchant vessels that sailed into Savannah's harbor.

📷 RIVER STREET, SAVANNAH

When you arrive in Savannah, your explorations will undoubtedly take you to River Street. It is vibrant and alive, full of tourists, artists, street performers, and young students. The fast-flowing Savannah River parallels the street, past wide sidewalks, parks, and street art that create a welcoming atmosphere. Capitalizing on this inimitable draw are the shops and restaurants that line the street, providing innumerable options for the constant influx of visitors. River Street is not on the bluff, which means you will typically find yourself

on steep stone steps when coming or going from this area of the city. For those with mobility issues, there are elevators available. Once you are down at the water, you can take your time and soak it all in. The boat traffic is nearly constant, as are the cars that rumble over the cobblestone streets. The hustle and bustle of this area stands in stark contrast to the peaceful vibes that exude from other parts of the historic district, but if you like to shop and eat, River Street should be on your itinerary.

SAVANNAH RIVERBOAT CRUISES, SAVANNAH

Most visitors stroll down River Street and take in the views of the Savannah River as it rapidly flows past the bustling downtown. But an even better way to enjoy the river is to explore it by boat. It might not be the cheapest thing you do during your stay in Savannah, but a cruise provides patrons with an intimate look at the Savannah waterfront, as well as other nearby areas. Mix in live entertainment and satisfying dining, and you get a recipe for a memorable day on the water. The boats leave directly from the center of River Street, making it especially convenient to add to your day's itinerary. *savannahriver boat.com, (912) 232-6404*

Cobblestones and streetcar tracks give a glimpse into the history of River Street.

The Cathedral of St. John the Baptist offers beautiful architecture.

📷 CATHEDRAL OF SAINT JOHN THE BAPTIST, SAVANNAH

The oldest Roman Catholic Church in Georgia is an architectural masterpiece, featuring beautiful stained-glass windows everywhere you look. Originally built in 1876, much of the structure was destroyed by fire, leading to a rebuild completed in 1900. Visit in the early morning and the light streaming through the windows will invoke a sense of awe no matter what your religious preference. Stroll in, sit down in a pew, and gaze up at the impossibly high ceiling, complete with ornate woodwork that invokes wonder and astonishment. The detailed craftsmanship and vivid paintings grab your eye, but the serenity calms your soul. Stroll slowly, sit pensively, speak quietly, and enjoy fully. *savannahcathedral.org, (912) 233-4709*

📷 FORSYTH PARK, SAVANNAH

Plenty of visitors explore the squares of Savannah without ever stepping foot in this 30-acre park. Perhaps that's because it is a bit of a stroll from other areas of the historic district. But it is worth the exercise because the paths, trees, fountain, and ubiquitous moss coalesce into a visually striking location. There's a farmers' market every Saturday and other festivals throughout the year. A playground will occupy the kids and the picturesque fountain, modeled after similar ones in Cuzco, Peru, will grab the eye of almost everyone, especially shutterbugs.

CITY MARKET, SAVANNAH

Shopping, eating, people-watching, and live music—this is City Market, which once served as Savannah's central marketplace in the 1700s and now injects a pulse into the historic district. Some mismanagement and demolition of historical buildings in the 1950s had Savannah's residents up in arms, which fueled a community-led movement toward the preservation of this and other historical areas throughout the city. The result? A once again thriving area that serves as a hub for food, art, and plenty of imbibing. As day turns to night, families with children give way to those seeking entertainment and nightlife. Patrons walk their drinks

The City Market offers dining, shopping, and some great nightlife.

DID YOU KNOW? One of the largest Saint Patrick's Day parades in the entire country takes place in Savannah every year. The weekend-long festival ensures plenty of merriment for the hundreds of thousands who flock to the streets and the bars throughout the city.

from bar to bar until the wee hours of the morning as the latest hits spill from the open doors and windows. At 3 a.m. things wind down and the streets become quiet for a few hours until the rising sun ushers in a new day of activity and merrymaking. *savannahcitymarket.com, (912) 232-4903*

Live oak trees are everywhere in Forsyth Park.

LEOPOLD'S ICE CREAM, SAVANNAH

If an ice cream parlor can be famous, then Leopold's is to Georgia what De Niro is to Hollywood. Its reputation is world-wide, and it is frequented by A-list celebrities who are often filming movies along the Georgia coast. Founded in 1919, the Broughton Street icon has a retro feel to accompany the more than 28 flavors of ice cream made every day, batch by batch. Current owner Stratton Leopold spent almost 40 years working on major motion pictures and that influence can be found throughout the shop. In fact, the entire place was designed by Dan Lamino, an Academy Award–nominated set designer. No matter what is on your itinerary, don't leave Savannah until you try a scoop or two. Be warned though, on a warm day the line might be out the door and down the block! *leopoldsicecream .com, (912) 234-4442.*

GHOST TOURS, SAVANNAH

Perhaps the trying times early in its history—times full of destruction and despair—contributed to the countless tales of ghosts and hauntings throughout Savannah. Visitors can choose from a large selection of ghost tours, which can be fascinating even if you're not convinced of the supernatural. For a bit of history, architecture, and some exercise, make reservations for the **Savannah Ghostwalker Tour** (ghostwalkertours .com, 912-662-0155). This tour is a bit more intimate and provides you with history, ghost stories, and your own equipment to detect paranormal activity. If you'd prefer a bit of a buzz from your own spirits before you take on the creepy spirits of yesteryear, then the **Creepy Crawl Haunted Pub Tour** (savannahtours.com, 912-238-3843) has you covered. You'll visit four local bars and walk through several haunted sites, all while sipping

One of the most famous ice cream parlors in the South can be found in Savannah.

Wormsloe offers fantastic photographic opportunities.

on your favorite drink. Yes, part of the Savannah experience for many is taking advantage of its incredibly lax open container law.

📷 WORMSLOE HISTORIC SITE, SAVANNAH

One of the most picturesque locations in all of Georgia is found at the tree-lined entrance to this historic plantation located just south of the city. Simply passing under the old stone archway and onto the grounds gives you the feeling you are somewhere steeped in history. Stately and intricate live oak trees tower over the mile-long road leading to the plantation, with extensive Spanish moss providing a stately feel that words cannot express. Numerous trails run throughout the site, affording visitors access to beautiful grounds and scenic views of the Isle of Hope. The home, originally constructed in 1745, is now in ruins, but don't let

that dissuade you from spending a few hours exploring the grounds and museum. *gastateparks.org/wormsloe*, *(912) 353-3023*

🦬 SKIDAWAY ISLAND STATE PARK, SAVANNAH

Hiking, camping, paddling, and rental cabins are the highlights of this state park that sits to the southeast of Savannah. Its close proximity to beautiful locations such as Wormsloe State Historic Site make it a particularly intriguing option for those who want to explore the Savannah area and spend plenty of time outside. The Sandpiper Trail takes you over boardwalks, bridges, salt marshes, and plenty of forests. If you'd rather give your upper body a workout, head out in a canoe or kayak to explore the marsh and look for dolphins and ospreys. *gastateparks.org/skidaway island, (912) 598-2300*

The late day sun casts an orange glow across the marsh at Skidaway.

COASTAL GEORGIA GREENWAY, SAVANNAH

If you'd like to trade in the sounds of traffic and internal combustion engines for the sanctity of nature and gentle rolling of your bicycle tires, then the burgeoning trail system that runs from South Carolina to Florida is just what you need. Still under construction, there are plenty of paths that allow you to walk, run, or bike your way from Savannah down the coast, ending in Saint Mary's. One day the greenway will link all of the existing segments together, but there are already miles and miles of completed trails throughout the communities along the coast. Check the website to plan your explorations. *coastalgeorgia greenway.org*

TYBEE ISLAND

Savannah isn't quite on the coast, so if you are looking for sand and

DID YOU KNOW? Georgia was originally conceived as a prison colony for debtors from England. It was spearheaded by James Oglethorpe, the English parliamentarian, who wanted more humane conditions for debtors who suffered in England's filthy prison system.

that laid-back beach vibe, a quick ride out Highway 80 takes you to the small but charming Tybee Island. Located where the Savannah River finally meets the Atlantic Ocean after its 301-mile journey down the eastern border of Georgia, Tybee is a throwback to beach towns before they were transformed into tourist traps with IMAX theaters and kitschy theme parks. This area brings visitors from near and far who want to soak up some rays and frolic in the surf. Don't be surprised to see license plates from New York and

Dining in Savannah

There is no doubt that Savannah offers a range of dining options that will satisfy practically any craving you might have. Modern restaurants on the forefront of the culinary world are opening often, including critically acclaimed locations such as **The Grey** (thegreyrestaurant.com, 912-662-5999) and **45 Bistro** (45bistro.com, 912-234-3111).

Few will argue that one of the most iconic locations is the **Olde Pink House** (planters innsavannah.com, 912-232-4286). This pink mansion was constructed in 1771 and is one of the few Savannah buildings to survive the fire of 1796. Though it has served several purposes over the past two centuries, it is now a popular restaurant that serves Southern and Lowcountry fare in a fine dining setting. The art, chandeliers, and overall craftsmanship give a glimpse into the past while the food makes you thoroughly appreciate just how good the culinary world has become.

If the weather is nice and you are looking for a view, the outdoor patio of **Tubby's Seafood** (tubbysseafood.com, 912-233-0770) is the place to be. Live music, fresh seafood, cold drinks, and al fresco dining usually have people lining up on the staircase that rises from the sidewalk below. You'll pay a bit extra for the scenery, but the food is solid and the people watching is first rate. Overlooking River Street and the Savannah River, you can munch on fried shrimp and gaze upon passing cargo ships that dwarf the nearby buildings and hotels.

If Savannah gets a little too crowded for you and you want to enjoy a peaceful meal with an amazing view, visit **The Wyld Dock Bar** (thewylddockbar.com, 912-692-1219) where you can dine on casual seafood while soaking in the expansive view of the scenic marsh. Popular with the locals, the dock sits right over the water, creating an atmosphere that coalesces nicely with the fresh seafood on your plate. The menu changes based on the availability of the locally caught seafood, ensuring a level of quality and freshness that many restaurants fail to match.

beyond, especially in the early spring when it has warmed up in Georgia but there is still snow on the ground farther north. Beauty and history converge on this 3.2-square-mile piece of waterfront paradise, providing visitors with the chance to take a stroll on the beach, dine at a variety of restaurants, and visit a historical site that played a key role in the Civil War. Enjoy your time on Tybee and soak in the relaxed vibe of "Savannah's beach." While many visitors will simply make it a day trip from Savannah, there is something alluring about spending a few days lounging in the sand, bicycling around the island, dining on fresh seafood, and having a few drinks with the locals. *tybee island.com, (912) 786-5444*

TYBEE ISLAND PIER AND PAVILION, TYBEE ISLAND

Tybee certainly has its share of magnificent beach homes and condos, but it's the cottages nestled in neighborhoods off the main road that add to the charm of this small town. Not far from these neighborhoods sits a large fishing pier that that stretches into the Atlantic. This provides ample opportunities for fishing,

The Tybee Island Pier is a great place to get out over the water and enjoy the scenery.

people-watching, or simply enjoying the sound of the crashing waves 20 feet below. A cash-only bar, ice cream shop, and take-away café sit at the entrance to the pier, offering the bare necessities to the many beachgoers who pass through the area. Nearby shops and restaurants mean you can park once and not move your car for the rest of the day.

TYBEE ISLAND MARINE SCIENCE CENTER, TYBEE ISLAND

Near the pier and pavilion you will find this small but informative educational center which houses interactive exhibits about the ecological diversity of the Georgia coast. Visitors have the chance to go on educational walks through the marsh, on the beach, or get up close with a way-too-cute sea turtle. Construction is underway on a new and larger center which will showcase even more interactive

opportunities for visitors. *tybee marinescience.org, (912) 786-5917*

FORT SCREVEN, TYBEE ISLAND

If you want to get off the beach for a little while, head north to broaden your historical perspective of this part of Georgia. Fort Screven was established in 1898 as a component of America's coastal defense system. American troops occupied the area throughout the Spanish American War as well as World Wars I and II, primarily due to the importance of preserving the shipping lanes in the Savannah River. After its closure in 1947, the fort's structures were preserved, including the Battery Garland, which now houses the island's museum.

TYBEE ISLAND LIGHT STATION, TYBEE ISLAND

Near Fort Screven is the Tybee Island Light Station, the oldest and tallest lighthouse in Georgia. Your heart will be pumping after the 178 steps to the top, but the view of Tybee and the Georgia coast is well worth it. *tybee lighthouse.org, (912) 786-5801*

FORT PULASKI NATIONAL MONUMENT, TYBEE ISLAND

If you love history, lighthouses, or both, continue up Highway 80 to Fort Pulaski, which is managed by the National Park Service. This fortification was commissioned in the early 1800s and took several decades to build. Initially occupied by Confederate forces, the Union army set up

A pelican floats through the blue sky above Tybee Island.

artilleries on Tybee Island and began bombarding the structure with a

The Tybee Island Lighthouse offers panoramic views of the Georgia coastline.

Dining in Tybee

After all your exploring, you're going to be hungry. Fortunately there are plenty of great restaurants throughout the island. Down near the pier there are several blocks of dive bars, seafood restaurants, and old hotels that have been renovated to meet the expectations of modern travelers. After lying on the beach all day, you might be fine grabbing a slice of pizza and a cold drink at one of the local watering holes. However, if you like views and fresh air with your seafood, try **Bubba Gumbo's** (tybeebubbags.com, 912-786-4445), an unpretentious little spot on the marsh with freshly caught seafood, refreshing drinks, and some live music.

If you're in search of breakfast, **The Breakfast Club** (thebreakfastclubtybee.com, 912-786-5984) serves as a great start to your day. In addition to your typical dishes, you will find more unique concoctions such as the Smoked Salmon Omelet.

rifled cannon, the first of its kind. Though the walls were more than seven feet thick, a 30-hour bombardment of rifled projectiles breached the wall and the Confederates eventually surrendered.

Visitors can explore the fort and then head out along the path to see the picturesque **Cockspur Island** **Lighthouse**, which was built in 1839 and has facilitated safe passage for countless ships. *nps.gov/fopu, (912) 786-5787*

🐃 HARRIS NECK NATIONAL WILDLIFE REFUGE, TOWNSEND

One of only 18 sites along the **Colonial Coast Birding Trail**, this national

Cockspur Island Lighthouse offers some history and plenty of beauty.

Visitors are always treated to a sunrise on the Georgia coast.

wildlife refuge offers more than fifteen miles of roads and trails that wind through marsh and woods. You're certain to spot a large variety of birds, as 342 species have been seen within its borders since it was formed in 1962. If you're lucky, you might also spot an alligator or two.

BLACKBEARD ISLAND NATIONAL WILDLIFE REFUGE

Not far from Savannah sit thousands of acres set aside for wildlife and migratory birds. Many a story has been told about the treasure that the legendary pirate Blackbeard once buried on this island, although none has been found. Accessible only by boat, this untouched oasis of salt marsh, forest, and sandy beaches is not crowded. If you want to see what the Georgia coast looked like before homes were built and asphalt was poured, then this is a perfect spot to get away from it all. If you'd prefer to have a guide take you to the island, you can't go wrong with **SouthEast Adventure Outfitters** (southeast adventure.com, 912-638-6732).

SAPELO ISLAND

Not too far from the bustling, vibrant city of Savannah lies an island rich with history, beauty, and seclusion. This state-protected barrier island is only accessible by ferry and many head here to get lost and connect with the majesty of nature. Small roads and trails snake throughout Sapelo, leading to historic ruins, an old lighthouse, and the secluded **Cabretta Island Campground**, which has bathrooms, flushable toilets, and hot showers. If you want to spend an evening or two under the stars, this is the place for you. Stroll over to the beach from the campground and discover tide pools, shells, driftwood, and perhaps a horseshoe crab.

If you are looking for more luxurious accommodations and have at least 15 friends willing to pitch in, you can rent the **Reynolds Mansion** (gastateparks.org/ReynoldsMansion, 912-437-3224), which is also a main draw for visitors to the island. This 13-bedroom estate features beguiling architecture, an extensive library, and even a bowling alley. Originally

A fantastic sunrise lights up the beach on Sapelo Island.

The Reynolds Mansion offers architecture and history.

erected in 1810 by the architect Thomas Spalding, the tabby construction was no match for Union cannons during the Civil War. It fell into ruin until it was rebuilt by an automotive engineer, who sold it to tobacco heir Richard Reynolds. Upon his death, the Georgia Department of Natural Resources took over the care and management of the mansion and surrounding island. Groups of 16 to 29 people can reserve the mansion for two or more nights of pampering and relaxation. Tours of the mansion are also available with advance notice, including a bus tour that takes advantage of the limited road system. There are also guided beach walks and interpretive tours of the mansion.

Another fascinating aspect of Sapelo Island is the living history present in the small community of **Hog Hammock.** Like most of the coast, the island was once a plantation farmed by slaves. The Gullah Geechee people are descendants from Central and West Africans who were brought to the United States to work in the coastal areas of Georgia, South Carolina, and northern Florida. Hailing from different countries and cultural backgrounds, the slaves worked alongside each other for many years, eventually forming their own language and cultural traditions. Those traditions continue today in the 434-acre Hog Hammock, where approximately 50 descendants of the Gullah Geechee slaves still reside. This tight-knit community has a single small store with the basic necessities. Everything else requires a ferry ride to the mainland, including school for the island's children.

While some visitors might take a stroll through the quiet streets of Hog Hammock, others might be interested in the research facilities located here. **Sapelo Island National Estuarine Research Reserve** (sapelonerr.org, 912-485-2251) and **University of Georgia Marine Institute** (ugami.uga.edu, 912-485-2221) are both located on the island, facilitating a constant influx of researchers, including ecologists, biologists, and historians.

Gray's Reef National Marine Sanctuary (graysreef.noaa.gov, 912-598-2345) can be found 19 miles off the coast of Sapelo Island and is a haven for fishermen as well as divers who want to explore the twisting rocky ledges and flat uninterrupted areas of sandy bottom.

If you visit both Sapelo and Cumberland Islands, you will notice some similarities with how beautifully they are preserved, as well as the priority of nature over development. Both have stunning, stately mansions, are accessible only by ferry, and have thousands of acres of live oaks, undeveloped shoreline, and abundant wildlife. While Cumberland is federally managed, Sapelo is almost wholly owned and managed by the state of Georgia.

Whatever your goal, stepping off of the ferry to Sapelo Island is like taking a step back in time. It's a place where you can explore, uninterrupted, for hours at a time. It's a place where there are far more animals than people. It's a place where you can stroll the beach and get a glimpse of the world just how the settlers saw it, hundreds of years ago. It's a place to get away from the hustle and bustle of civilization, if only for a day.

THE GOLDEN ISLES

Georgia's coast has plenty of destinations for you to explore, including four Golden Isles that showcase the immense beauty of the Georgia coast, without the bright lights and

Sidney Lanier Bridge provides access between Brunswick and Jekyll Island.

typical tourist attractions that can proliferate many coastal communities. These four slivers of land: **Saint Simons Island, Sea Island, Jekyll Island,** and **Little Saint Simons Island,** are located close to one another and are part of a larger chain of barrier islands that stretch from Savannah to Jacksonville. Each of these islands has a distinct feel, stemming from the style of development, as well as the people who flock to the shores. One ecologically and aesthetically beautiful thing about Georgia's coast is the harmony between the Atlantic Ocean and the 378,000 acres of marshlands that span the coastline in a four- to six-mile swath. A vast array of marine flora and fauna thrive within this region, inhabiting small, tucked away inlets as well as larger

waterways that lead to the vast Atlantic. This is a paradise for naturalists and photographers. Speaking of, shutterbugs will appreciate that the orientation of the entire coast ensures a daily sunrise over the ocean, no matter the time of the year. The close proximity of the four Golden Isles means that visitors can experience any and all of the unique locations with relative ease, allowing for a coastal visit that is truly unique and immensely satisfying. Both Sea Island and Little Saint Simons Island are privately-owned, exclusive resorts with no public access. Because of this, they won't be covered in detail here in the book. However, if you want to experience a luxurious beach vacation, both islands offer incredible settings with fine dining and lavish amenities. *goldenisles.com, (912) 638-9014*

BRUNSWICK

The city of Brunswick provides easy access to Sea Island, Saint Simon's Island, and Jekyll Island. Similar to the much larger Savannah, the city sits slightly inland from the coast and is laid out in a series of squares with many parks interspersed throughout the downtown. The numerous waterways and deep water of Fancy Bluff Creek provide easy access for the fleet of shrimp boats to reach the Atlantic.

The city is steeped in history, dating back to the 1700s when the first Europeans arrived and established a 1,000-acre tobacco plantation. Growth here was slower than in Savannah, which benefitted from a large shipping lane provided by the Savannah River. Nevertheless, Brunswick's deep-water port and close proximity to the sea have created opportunities for commerce, including shipyards, naval stores, and now agricultural exports.

One thing that will never change is how much people love the beach, and so tourism is one of the main industries for Brunswick. The downtown has a variety of shops and squares, including the historic **Hanover Park** that sits just a block from the Old City Hall. This park is one of the few that has retained its size and shape since its inception in the late 1800s.

In addition to the alluring islands that are a short drive from downtown Brunswick, the city also offers the **Hofwyl-Broadfield Plantation** (gastateparks.org/hofwylbroadfield plantation, 912-264-7333). A rice plantation in the early 1800s, this property provides a glimpse into the "rice coast" that was pervasive throughout the South Carolina and Georgia coastlines during that period. There is

Historic Hanover Park offers a glimpse into Brunswick's past.

The pier on Saint Simons Island is frequented by visitors and fishermen.

a museum and nature trail to explore, and it also serves as a stop on the Colonial Coast Birding Trail.

If all your explorations leave you feeling hungry, stop by the **Indigo Coastal Shanty** (indigocoastalshanty .com, 912-265-2007), which has the laid-back beach vibe atmosphere you want with your coastal cuisine. The eclectic restaurant offers a variety of fresh fish, as well as some land fare sure to satisfy any appetite.

If you prefer drinking over eating, **Richland Rum** (richlandrum.com, 229-887-3537) has you covered. Being the only single-estate rum distillery in the United States means this distinctive farm and distillery creates and utilizes every single component of the rum-making process on location.

SAINT SIMONS ISLAND

Shrimp boats slowly cruise by, making their way out to the Atlantic where they will haul in hundreds of pounds of tasty crustaceans to ship all over the world. A warm, gentle breeze blows in off the water, rustling the Spanish moss that hangs from virtually every live oak on the island. Residents and visitors mill about, walking or bicycling to the beach or to grab a bite to eat. It is a laid-back lifestyle, an alluring combination of great food, beautiful beaches, and friendly people. Twelve miles in length by three miles in width, Saint Simons is located a few short miles from Brunswick and the mainland. A drive along the causeway takes you over creeks and estuaries, eventually depositing you right into the heart of downtown. Of course, this little slice of paradise hasn't always catered to the beach lovers of the southeast. After the

Saint Simons visitors gaze across Saint Simons Sound towards Jekyll Island.

Light streams through the massive oak trees near Sea Island.

A sunset lights up the sky near downtown Saint Simons.

American Revolution, the island was comprised of cotton plantations that thrived until the Civil War. From that point forward, the plantations languished, and small farms dotted the landscape. In the late 1800s a lighthouse was constructed, and with it followed the beginning of tourism to the island. Then a small amusement park was built, followed by hotels, houses, and restaurants. In 1924, a causeway opened that gave easy access to the beaches of the island, precipitating a boom of construction and tourism.

While all of the barrier islands are popular vacation destinations, Saint Simons is perhaps the most developed island along the Georgia coast. The city has done a nice job of curtailing poor planning or unsightly structures, creating a destination that has many intangibles that coalesce into a highly enjoyable experience. In other words: it just feels right. Incredibly old trees line the roads, and charming neighborhoods are in abundance as you make the drive in from Brunswick. Once downtown, you find street after street full of shops, restaurants, boutique hotels, and art galleries. This is not a sleepy beach town—it is a culturally rich destination that provides easy access to the coast, but with plenty to do if you don't want to get covered in sand. *explorestsimons island.com*

NEPTUNE PARK, SAINT SIMONS ISLAND

After you arrive in the downtown area, a good place to begin your exploration is Neptune Park. Situated right on the water, the park is adjacent to the Saint Simons Pier, a concrete structure that stretches out into Saint Simons Sound and provides easy access for fishing and sightseeing. The park has several attractions worth a look. Miniature golf, a pool, splash pad, and a large playground all provide plenty of entertainment for the whole family.

📷 SAINT SIMONS LIGHTHOUSE AND MUSEUM, SAINT SIMONS ISLAND

A short walk from the park takes you to this historic structure that also features a museum. Stroll through the museum and learn about the beginning of the island, the settlers who passed through, and all the technology used in a lighthouse. Afterward, ascend the 104-foot structure for a fantastic view of the water and

The lighthouse and museum offer history with a view.

Dining on Saint Simons Island

If you start getting hungry, there are many wonderful restaurants for every price point and type of cuisine. Since you're on the coast, you would be remiss if you didn't sample some fresh seafood and perhaps a tropical beverage or two. If you want to go a little upscale, then the **Georgia Sea Grill** (georgiaseagrill.com, 912-638-1197) is a solid option. Located on the edge of the historic district, the menu offers a range of fresh seafood cooked with a creative flair. When in doubt, choose the grilled scallops. For a more laid-back setting, check out either **Iguana's Seafood** (iguanasseafood.com, 912-638-9650) or the **Half Shell** (thehalfshellssi.com, 912-268-4241). Both have outdoor patios, some good beer on tap, and lots of people-watching to go along with the fresh seafood. Iguana's has won numerous awards for their fried shrimp, and it is indeed excellent. Speaking of awards, **Southern Soul BBQ** (southernsoulbbq.com, 912-638-7685) has won a ton of them, and for good reason. The BBQ coming out of this converted gas station is world-class.

surrounding island. *coastalgeorgia history.com, 912-634-7090*

SAINT SIMONS TROLLEY TOUR, SAINT SIMONS ISLAND

There is plenty of history around the island, and you can either explore it yourself or get ferried from location to location on a comfortable trolley. Along with easy access to some of the most interesting locations all over the island, there is a local historian who can answer almost any question you have about the area. The daily tour departs at 11 a.m. and you can reserve your spot through the website. *stsimonstours.com, (912) 638-8954*

BEACHES, SAINT SIMONS ISLAND

The beaches of the island are constantly changing due to the fluctuating tides along the coast. During certain times of the year, the tides in Georgia can vary by seven feet or more, changing the coastline dramatically and providing (or removing) access to a lot of sand for people to enjoy. The coast experiences two high tides and two low tides every day, so check the charts and plan accordingly if you want to maximize your time for exploration and recreation. There are several public access areas around the island, and **East Beach** is one of the largest and most popular for exploring. Another interesting location is **Gould's Inlet**, which has a small parking area and offers tide pools, views towards Sea Island, as well as the occasional surfer tackling swells approaching the shoreline.

SOUTHEAST ADVENTURE OUTFITTER, SAINT SIMONS ISLANDS

The Georgia marsh is the second largest in the United States and features a rich but delicate ecosystem of plants, aquatic animals, and birds. There are many ways to get up close and personal with the natural beauty surrounding Saint Simon's Island, but perhaps the most engaging is a kayak or stand-up paddleboard tour that gets you out in the water. Southeast Adventure Outfitter runs daily kayak tours throughout the "trails"

A winding creek passes through the marsh on Jekyll Island.

of the Georgia coast, allowing you to explore the broad creeks that turn into narrow waterways, winding their way throughout the estuarial system. Birds, dolphins, turtles, and a host of other wildlife add to the ambiance and contribute to a memorable outing. For those that want to stay absolutely dry, there are also a selection of boat cruises to choose from. *south eastadventure.com, (912) 638-6732*

JEKYLL ISLAND

Ask almost anyone who lives in Georgia, and they will tell you that Jekyll is a special place. Almost ten miles long but under two miles in width, this wonderfully preserved barrier island has a near perfect blend of environmental beauty and modern amenities. As with much of the coast, this island was originally settled by British colonists and at one time served as a massive plantation situated on the Atlantic Ocean. Inevitably, the Civil War changed things and it evolved

The Milky Way offers a serene contrast with Driftwood Beach.

into a resort destination, originally as a hunting club for the nation's elite (the Rockefellers had a "cottage" on the island that can still be toured) before being sold to the state of Georgia for use as a state park. Soon after, the Jekyll Island Authority was formed to manage the island and preserve the delicate balance between the natural resources and public use.

Today the island is thriving, with more than ten miles of beachfront and 25 miles of bike paths that attract visitors from across the United States and beyond. The island has been beautifully preserved and features large swaths of forest and beachfront that cannot be developed. In fact, 65 percent of the island sits undeveloped, helping to preserve the natural habitat for sea turtles and other species that call the island home. Speaking of development, while there are numerous hotels and condos on the island, they are a far cry from Miami Beach or the Florida Gulf. The tallest building is only 50 feet in height, ensuring a desirable balance between lodging and aesthetics that preserve nature's beauty. Though the mantra for this oasis is "nature first" there is still plenty to do. Biking, hiking, golfing, and eating are just a few things that might get you out of your sand chair and exploring the far reaches of the island. *jekyll island.com, (912) 635-3636*

📷 🌳 DRIFTWOOD BEACH, JEKYLL ISLAND

One of the most famous beaches in the United States sits at the northern end of Jekyll Island. While there is occasional driftwood that washes up on the shore, some might feel the name is a misnomer. The location is actually famous for the gnarled, weathered trees that protrude from the sand and rocks. The slow, steady, and unending erosion of this stretch of sand has claimed the lives of many trees, but their smooth weathered bark remains. The changing tides provide fleeting access to many of the trees for those who want to climb, photograph, or hang a hammock. The beach is iconic and provides an experience unlike anywhere else in Georgia. Walk amongst the trees, listen to the water crash against their exposed roots, and appreciate the powerful beauty of nature. The expanse of sand almost looks like a tree graveyard, with toppled trunks that stretch hundreds of yards down the coast. The mix of oak and pine trees is unique, some on their sides and others sticking straight out of the sand, looking almost alive if it wasn't for the complete absence of leaves.

The beach is incredibly picturesque as the sun rises over the Atlantic,

A fishing trawler collects marine life from the Georgia marsh.

Beautiful old trees are found all over the Georgia coast.

bringing photographers from all over the world to capture their silhouettes against the pink hues on the horizon. Hurricane Matthew took its toll on the area, washing away some of the most famous trees and toppling others, but the constantly changing and eroding shoreline is part of the draw to this stretch of sand, and is a must-visit if you are in the area. Multiple paths lead to the beach with parking along the road, and the area is large enough that you can find a spot of your very own to relax and soak it all in.

DRIFTWOOD BEACH HORSEBACK RIDES

If you'd like to visit Driftwood Beach using a very unique form of transportation, then check out the horseback rides offered by **Three Oaks Farm**. Available for riders ages three and older, the journey takes you through the live oak trees and out onto the sand where you can experience the beauty of the crashing waves, the warm breeze, and the weathered trees of the beach, all astride a very well-behaved horse. Numerous rides are offered, including sunset and moonlight rides. *threeoaksfarm.org, (912) 635-9500*

BIKING JEKYLL ISLAND

If you prefer a different type of transportation, Jekyll Island is a bicyclist's nirvana. Miles of well-planned and flat paths snake around the island, providing easy access for visitors no matter their age or fitness. More than 25 miles of biking trails are a nod to the conservationist philosophy that guides the decision-making on the island. From virtually anywhere on Jekyll, you can hop on a trail and bike to any other location with relative ease. Explore the beach, the marsh, the historic district, and everywhere in between, all with a breeze in your face and the heartening knowledge that you are getting a little healthier in the process. If you don't want to bring your own bike, there are several locations that rent them. **Jekyll Wheels** (912-635-5185) has a nice selection for all abilities, including a trike option for those who don't trust their balance.

If you want to plan a day of biking, start in the historic district and follow the many paths by the beautiful cottages and live oaks. Take the trail over to the Jekyll Island Beach Village, an assortment of shops and restaurants next to the ocean. You can stay north on the path for a while, hugging the coast and devouring scenic vistas over the Atlantic before the trail moves inland a bit. From there you eventually end up at the iconic Driftwood Beach. If the tide is out, the sand is firm enough for you to head out and bike through the graveyard of gnarled trees, eventually rounding the northern tip of the island and putting you at Clam Creek. Here you will find a large fishing pier and picnic area that looks across the sound toward Saint Simons Island. Next you can take one of many paths that bring you back to the heart of Jekyll. Note that some of the paths aren't paved and will take you through the forest, which can be a really intriguing way to explore the middle of the island. You will find thick groves of live oak trees along with Spanish moss floating in the sea breeze.

GEORGIA SEA TURTLE CENTER, JEKYLL ISLAND

You'll be hard-pressed to find anyone who doesn't love these harmless creatures of the sea. Sadly, only one in 4,000 lives to be a reproductive adult, placing every species on the federal endangered or threatened list. Nesting season along the Georgia

Exploring Jekyll by bicycle is a wonderful way to get off the beaten path.

The Georgia Sea Turtle Center provides medical care to injured turtles.

coast goes from May to August, and five different species of sea turtles use the Georgia beaches to nest and lay hundreds of thousands of eggs every year. These include loggerhead, green, leatherback, Kemp's ridley, and the hawksbill. The turtles range in size and population, but the most

There are five different species of sea turtles that nest along the Georgia coast.

common species of turtles found along the Georgia coast are loggerhead sea turtles. The largest of all hard-shelled turtles, the loggerheads have big heads, powerful jaws, and a reddish-brown shell. Males can weigh upward of 250 pounds and can grow three feet or longer. The loggerhead sea turtle's population faces constant challenges due to natural causes such as beach erosion along with manmade issues, including shrimp trawling and coastal development. The turtles come ashore to deposit their eggs in a nest in the sand, and around 60 days later the hatchlings emerge from the nest and start the dangerous journey back to the ocean. The hatchlings generally emerge at night and follow the light of the moon and its reflection off the ocean water. It is crucial that no street lights, lanterns, bonfires, or other manmade lights distract the hatchlings from the guiding light of the moon. The lucky ones who make it to the sea can live from 50 to 80 years, or even more.

You can see and learn about these marine turtles year-round at the non-profit Georgia Sea Turtle Center situated in the middle of the island. The center pledges to "Rehabilitate.

Research. Educate" and provides a variety of opportunities for the public to get involved in that mission. If you want to do your part, simply visit their discovery center, as the price of admission will go toward the protection of these aquatic animals. Visitors are treated to an educational experience that features multiple exhibits, including the on-site hospital where all kinds of turtles are fed and rehabilitated due to injury. As of 2019, the center has rescued and released well over 500 sea turtles. *gstc.jekyllisland .com, (912) 635-4444*

JEKYLL ISLAND HISTORIC DISTRICT

Before the state took over Jekyll Island in the mid-1950s, it was a hunting club for some of the wealthiest people in the United States. This exclusive retreat included the construction of large, beautiful buildings, which still remain. The present-day historic district is situated on a pristine part of the island full of stately live oak trees, creating a setting that looks like a scene out of a movie. The district isn't large, so its size allows visitors to take a leisurely stroll and marvel at the architecture. If you want deeper insight into the history of the island, as well as exclusive access to the inside of a few buildings, hop on the 90-minute tram tour that explores the 240 acres of the district.

JEKYLL ISLAND DOLPHIN TOURS

Sometimes a change in perspective can really open your eyes to the beauty of an area. Nobody will deny the beauty of Jekyll Island, but the waterways that surround it offer their own charm and scenery that should be experienced. On top of that, there are large populations of bottlenose

Dining on Jekyll Island

It wouldn't be a true escape to the beach if there weren't some great local options for fresh seafood and relaxing settings. While Jekyll might not have the same selection as Saint Simons Island, its more developed neighbor to the north, there are plenty of reasons to stay on the island in search of a meal. If you want a laid-back vibe with views of the beautiful estuary that separates Jekyll from the mainland, **Zachry's Riverhouse** (zachrys-restaurant.com, 912-265-9080) is a solid choice. Lots of fresh shrimp options are available, as well as fresh fish that arrives each day. Arrive by car, bicycle, or even boat, as the deck overlooks the marina.

If you're the type to seek out where the locals dine, **Driftwood Bistro** (driftwood bistro.com, 912-635-3588) should be at the top of your list. Nestled in with a resort full of small villas, the restaurant has a range of offerings that will satisfy those who aren't a fan of creatures that once resided in the water. But have no fear, because there is plenty on the menu for seafood lovers. Wild-caught shrimp is prevalent throughout, with the shrimp and grits being particularly popular. There is a bar and lounge on site as well, in case you want to grab a drink and plan your next day of adventure.

If you are looking for the best combination of views and food, and perhaps a bit of live music, **The Wharf** (jekyllwharf.com, 912-635-3612) is your spot. The entire restaurant literally sits on piers in the middle of the estuary, affording patrons a panoramic view of Fancy Bluff Creek and the mainland beyond. The menu has variety, and the prices are reasonable considering the idyllic setting. Come for the food and stick around for a drink and a constantly rotating lineup of live music.

The historic district on Jekyll Island is filled with architecture and natural splendor.

There are plenty of dolphins along the coast, and a tour can get you up close.

dolphins that feed throughout the fertile Georgia estuaries, creating a perfect opportunity for viewing and photography. During warmer weather, 90-minute tours leave daily from the wharf in the historic district. You will experience Jekyll in a very different way and are almost guaranteed to spot some dolphins as they frolic and feed along the coast. *captainphillip .com, (912) 635-3152*

SUMMER WAVES WATER PARK, JEKYLL ISLAND

Georgia can get hot, and not everyone wants to lay on the beach all day. The good news is that you can still keep cool without filling your beach bag with sand. Situated on the Jekyll River, Summer Waves Water Park is a popular destination for families during the warmer months of summer. Multiple water slides tower over the park, but if you prefer activities in a more low-key setting then the wave pool or half-mile lazy river should

suffice. With cabanas for rent and food on site, all you need is your towel and swimsuit. *(912) 635-2074*

CUMBERLAND ISLAND NATIONAL SEASHORE

For outdoor lovers, there is first Cumberland Island, and then everywhere else. With its stunning beauty and well-preserved shores, this island is one of the least-accessible places in Georgia. However, it is very, very much worth the effort. It is an island in the truest sense of the word, located seven miles from the mainland and only accessible by a ferry that makes two 90-minute round trips each day. When you step off the boat, you find yourself in a paradise that has remained relatively the same for hundreds, if not thousands, of years. There are some rudimentary unpaved roads, a few homes, some old buildings, and then 56 square miles of undisturbed natural grandeur. If you know anything at all about

The main road through the island is nothing more than a sandy path.

A wild horse trots slowly up the path near Dungeness.

A stunning sunset lights up the marsh.

batteries, Oglethorpe constructed **Dungeness,** a large hunting mansion that was formed with tabby concrete. This fascinating process involves the burning of oyster shells and then mixing the resulting lime with water, sand, ash, and broken oyster shells. It was used extensively by settlers up and down the coast due to an abundance of the necessary resources. After the Spanish were defeated, the island was left relatively uninhabited and the buildings ultimately disappeared. After the Revolutionary War ended, the plantation era began. Another large mansion, also named Dungeness, was constructed on the island along with several other buildings that facilitated the day-to-day operation of a large plantation. While citrus fruit and olives were planted and harvested, the primary export was Sea Island Cotton. This strain of cotton was highly desirable due to the long fibers and silky texture, and the market price reflected it.

Most visitors to the island spend the day, coming over in the morning and returning before the sun dips below the horizon. But if you would like to stay a bit longer, there are two options, depending primarily on your budget and thirst for the outdoors.

the island, you have probably heard about the wild horses that can be traced back to the mid-1700s. Over one hundred of these magnificent animals still freely roam the island, foraging on vegetation and strolling down the beach as the waves lap the shoreline. They are certainly photogenic, but keep a safe distance from these animals that can weigh well over a thousand pounds.

Like most of the Georgia coast, Cumberland Island was originally settled by the Spanish in the sixteenth century. Development was minimal until the eighteenth century, when British colonization spread throughout the region. General James Oglethorpe had two forts built on the island to protect it from Spanish-occupied Florida, a short distance to the south. In addition to the

GREYFIELD INN, CUMBERLAND ISLAND

The most convenient, and therefore expensive, choice of accommodation on the island is the immaculate Greyfield Inn, which once served as a retreat for the Carnegies in the early 1900s. The all-inclusive stay provides guests with three meals a day as well as unfettered access to sports, fishing, and the beaches. How remarkable is this hotel? Remarkable enough to be the location for John F. Kennedy Jr.'s wedding. For most

The Dungeness Ruins are well worth the visit, especially at night.

travelers it would be categorized as a serious splurge, but in many ways it is well worth it. You arrive by private ferry to the dock just down a path from the hotel. A short walk takes you under beautiful oak trees with Spanish moss adorning the sprawling branches. During the stroll from the dock it's likely you will spot the first of many wild horses during your stay on the island. Up the grand staircase and into the inn, a guide walks you through the main features of the grounds, pointing out the "Honest John" bar (fully stocked); the historic antiques; the first edition books that you can pull off the shelves and read (try that in a museum); as well as the bicycles, kayaks, beach equipment, towels, and a host of other necessities and luxuries that all come included with your stay. All of your food is also included, and if you arrive early in the day you can grab a picnic basket and head off to parts unknown to explore and have a bite to eat. Not a bad first stop is the beach, a short walk or bike ride away down a sandy path that is postcard-worthy. Walk through the dunes and grab a beach chair and umbrella before you sit and enjoy the wonderful isolation of the sandy shoreline. The rest of your stay can consist of guided walks (there are several every day), excellent meals, and perhaps a cocktail or two. In fact, simply lounging on one of the oversized porch swings and feeling the breeze fall across the large front porch is a few hours, or even half a day, well spent in this slice of paradise. *greyfieldinn.com, (904) 261-6408*

CAMPING CUMBERLAND

Understandably, not everyone wants to splurge on a hotel room and some would prefer to feel more connected with nature the entire time on the

The Greyfield Inn is worth the splurge, and it is the only lodging on the island.

island. For those who want to forego the return ferry and watch the sun set and then rise again the next morning, the only other option is to camp. Even if you don't like to camp, this might be the time to get outside of your comfort zone and crawl into a sleeping bag for the night. There are a variety many campsites, from rustic wilderness sites with no running water to more developed areas that offer showers (cold ones) and actual toilets. Mankind has survived without these kinds of creature comforts for many generations, so most of us can go one night in exchange for an experience that might last a lifetime. Camping is limited, so make your reservations well in advance. *nps.gov/cuis, (912) 882-4336.*

EXPLORING CUMBERLAND

Exploring the island is best done by foot or bicycle, since there is only one main road and very few vehicles. The island is teeming with wildlife that thrive within the protective borders of the National Seashore. In addition to the abundant horses, you might spot deer, wild turkey, sea turtles, otters, bobcats, and an armadillo or two. There is one main road that runs between the Dungeness ruins and Stafford Plantation, and it can be traversed easily with a bicycle. If you want to bring your own you have to schedule it in advance and pay a $10 surcharge in addition to the cost of the ferry, so some travelers decide to rent one from the ranger station on the island ($16 per day or $20 for overnight). If you would rather explore the island on foot, there are more than 50 miles of hiking trails that provide access to various parts of the maritime forests and seashore. They range in distance and intensity, ensuring there is something for everyone.

Cumberland Island isn't just a must-visit for anyone spending some time in Georgia, it is a must-visit for anyone exploring the United States. So unique is its combination of history, conservation, and beauty, that it evokes a sense of wonder and amazement for even the most worldly travelers. The interplay of the sun, tides, waves, live oaks, wild horses, and solitude creates an experience that will be remembered for a lifetime.

A simple sandy road leads visitors from the forest to the ocean.

INDEX